TEENAGERS EDUCATED
THE VILLAGE WAY

Friends of Yemin Orde
Supporting educational communities
for at-risk youth in Israel.

04. 2 9. 2014

www.yeminorde.org

CHAIM PERI

TEENAGERS EDUCATED
THE VILLAGE WAY

TEACHINGS FROM
YEMIN ORDE YOUTH VILLAGE
MT. CARMEL, ISRAEL

This World: The Values Network Publishing Group

P.O. Box 61

Englewood, NJ 07631

This World: The Values Network Publishing Group is owned and operated by This World: The Values Network (www.ThisWorld.us), a non-profit, 501-C-3 organization. The name and logo for This World are trademarked.

Printed in the United States of America

October 2011

10 9 8 7 6 5 4 3 2 1

ISBN: 978-257-06206-5

TABLE OF CONTENTS

FOREWORD

BY MICHA ODENHEIMER

This book is not a manual that can magically change educators, parents, adolescents, or the harsh realities of the world. But I believe that there is magic in this book—a deep and subtle magic that can shift our perspective and expand our consciousness so that educating becomes something different; the inherent pain involved transformed from the anguish of frustration to the comforting ache of growth. At its root, this magic is the magic of faith—faith that we have within ourselves what it takes to provide the guidance our children need in order to learn how to live in this world. It is the magic of faith in our teenagers and in the promise they carry within themselves, even at their most terrible moments. Ultimately, it is faith in the power of life.

There is a story told about one of the great Jewish spiritual masters who noticed that one of his students, who was sitting with the rest of his disciples on a Sabbath eve, had a terrible pain in his eyes. As the others watched, the master walked over and placed his hands over the eyes of the disciple, who was writhing in pain. Miraculously, the disciple's cries of pain ceased and his facial contortions were replaced by an expression of relief. Later, his friends demanded to know: had his pain really ceased at the touch of the teacher's hand? "No," the disciple said, "the pain didn't go away. But it became a completely different kind of pain."

My first meeting with Chaim Peri took place in November of 1990; I traveled to Addis Ababa, the capital city of Ethiopia, to interview Mengistu Haile Mariam, the brutal and desperate dictator who held the fate of 25,000 Ethiopian Jews in his hands. Rebel forces were gaining ground in their drive to oust Mengistu, and in the muddy streets of Addis Ababa, undercurrents of ethnic and political violence coursed just below the barely controlled surface of daily life. Israeli diplomats, doctors, and rescue workers flew in and out of the city, attending to the Ethiopian Jews who had evacuated their villages in the north and were now living in abject poverty as they awaited permission to immigrate. But what was an educator, the director of the near-legendary Yemin Orde Youth Village for teenagers in the north of Israel, doing in this harsh and unpredictable country?

If the Ethiopian parents and siblings of teenagers living at Yemin Orde were trapped in an impossible situation because of the survivalist manipulations of a failing communist dictator, Chaim wanted to investigate and to fight for them. If the younger brothers and sisters of his teenage charges were dying of preventable diseases and malnutrition, Chaim had to try to change the situation. At the very least, Chaim wanted see the situation with his own eyes and to keep a tide of consolation and hope flowing between the generations. In the hilltop compound of the American Association for Ethiopian Jews (the AAEJ), one of the Jewish organizations aiding the internal refugees, hundreds of men and women gathered in a dark, cavernous tent to see photographs of their children that Chaim had brought with him from Yemin Orde. Chaim carefully posted the photos on the canvas walls of the tent. As each parent located the image of his or her child, the tent, with its single light bulb, seemed to brighten with fresh radiance.

Chaim Peri conceives of the task of education in the broadest possible terms. Education is the process through which each generation becomes conscious of what is most essential, valuable and precious in life, and hands this legacy—human civilization itself, in all its possibility and power—to the next generation. The very act of taking responsibility, of attempting to influence historical events to the extent one is able, is, for Peri, inseparable from the educational task. When the opportunity to work with Chaim on this book came to me we could not work on it in a reflective seclusion from the world—during a sabbatical year or in the quiet of a library—but as life continued to froth and churn around us. At first, many of our meetings were in Chaim's office in the village. Constant interruptions from young people, counselors, and other staff forced us to seek other places to work. We talked and wrote in cafes, restaurants, lawyers' offices, and hotel lobbies in Tel Aviv, Jerusalem, Atlit, and Zichron Yaakov. And still the interruptions came fast and furious. A young person from the Village had gone missing for a few hours. A graduate—from a class that had matriculated five, ten or fifteen years before—might be having financial, career or marital problems. A group of orphans from the former Soviet Union, or the families of terror victims, or the children of foreign workers, had arrived at the village. Dr. Peri's days and the life of the Yemin Orde Youth Village are never routine. In order to gather stories I interviewed a number of Yemin Orde graduates, and saw and heard first hand how their experiences in the village were carved into their hearts. I spoke with many of the village staff to see how the insights of Yemin Orde's methods had filtered into their consciousness. The lessons to be absorbed from the village and its methods captivated my imagination.

Parenthood and education, in Chaim's teaching, are Siamese twins that cannot be separated. In order for education to succeed, it must be infused with the parental qualities of caring and emotional connection. In an age where boarding schools, orphanages and therapeutic centers have become increasingly obsessed with delving into the wounds of their young charges, foisting upon them uncountable hours of therapy, Chaim Peri has come along to say: Stop! "Treatment" serves a purpose, but it is not the be-all and end-all when seeking to help wounded young people heal. After all, no matter how much treatment a child receives, it can only occupy a fraction of a given day. What happens during the rest of the day? Unfortunately, at many such institutions, the rest of the day is viewed simply as dead time between therapy sessions—and this "child warehousing" is a recipe for failure. Because the children who end up at Yemin Orde—and other such centers—have experienced the worst life has to offer. Therapy alone cannot make them whole again. They need so much more. Kids who have been abandoned once (or twice, or three times) understand from painful personal experience that the future is certain to hold further abandonment.

But to this, Chaim Peri says: No! Educators must imbue the entire fabric of a child's life with meaning and structure—their approach must be holistic, not piecemeal. Only in this way can educators send wounded children the essential message that the cycle of being cast off is over. What happened in the past in not destined to happen again in the future. When these kids arrive on the doorsteps of places like Yemin Orde, their worlds are falling apart. If we wish to transform their brokenness, the world in which we educate them must be marked by wholeness and cohesion. Indeed, this essential fact holds true as much for teenagers whose pasts have been marked by unspeakable trauma as for adolescents from "normal" homes. This book examines and explains how educators can go about offering young people the cohesion they require.

INTRODUCTION

THE VILLAGE WAY

COHESIVE EDUCATIONAL ENVIRONMENTS FOR AT-RISK YOUTH

> *"Where is the wisdom we have lost in knowledge?*
> *Where is the knowledge we have lost in information?"*
> —T.S. Eliot

"*It takes a village to raise a child*" has been reintroduced into Western consciousness. This famous African proverb underscores humanity's longing for this lost village. There is nostalgia for the past when people lived in villages and tribal communities, surrounded by their extended families. A sense of coherence was naturally woven into the flow of life. Children grew and developed within a balanced arena, where parents and other significant adult figures modeled and imparted a coherent set of qualities, connections, skills and beliefs.

Yemin Orde, the Orde Wingate Youth Village on Mt. Carmel has developed an effective educational model titled *The Village Way*. Its objective is to reproduce the qualities and deep structures of the original village of humanity in today's educational environments. *The Village Way* is about endowing children with recognition and pride in their past, and a sense of direction and security about their future, while simultaneously building an awareness of personal strengths and limitations. This book tells the story of The Village Way's emergence as an educational methodology, presenting theory illustrated by personal narratives throughout the text.

A graphic scheme outlines *The Village Way* conceptual framework. It is there for the sake of clarity and accessibility, and highlights these guiding principles and major narratives. Both components comprise the 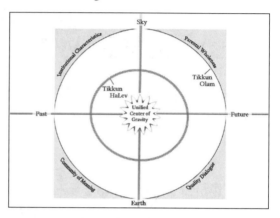 space-time continuum of our educational environment. We walk in the path of the renowned Kurt Z. Lewin and his 'force field analysis,' which follows the multiple influences that affect an individual child and cause him to move towards the goals of growth. *The Village Way* graphic schema illustrates both the educational environment as well as the dynamic reciprocity of content elements which is the essence of the youth village.

The origins of *The Village Way* lie in the philosophy of the founders of the Israeli Youth Villages. These educators have laid the foundations of a unique conceptual platform. They established character building educational environments in service of a great vision—the building of a homeland. In these Villages, youths discovered their strengths, developed self-esteem, and broadened their horizons. The ethos of this system had influence far beyond its confines. Its educators were considered homeland builders, and played a significant role in the young nation's formative years. For them, building a homeland was building a nation as well.

"A homeland," writes philosopher Jean Améry, is "the environment of our youth, and every person will become what he was in the first strata of his life. A *homeland* is the place where we internalize the nonverbal structure, the platform of a man's verbal and behavioral constitution for his entire life. Its significance means control over the dialectics of knowledge and awareness, of faith and trust."

From a young age, children often understand a great deal without being able to verbalize their comprehension. In the same manner, generative linguistics postulates that children grow into a mother tongue prior to learning its grammar. *The Village Way* seeks to become the 'inner grammar' of the educational environment into which a child grows. This 'inner grammar' is actually the blueprint of that essential homeland, into which the child *deserves* to grow.

The Village Way is about consolidating the different components that comprise educational entities into a unifying experience. Children and educators together inhabit this homeland in which language, spoken and unspoken, forms the foundation for a comprehensive and coherent place that encompasses the entire educational environment. This 'unifying experience' is created when children are enveloped in surroundings they understand that provide the foundation for psychological clarity, comprehension, loyalty, and values. It is this security and safety that will serve to guide them through the rest of their lives.

Yet today parts of that homeland of safety have descended into chaos. As a result, the opportunity for the child to fulfill his potential, connect to others, achieve autonomy, and have faith in the future are threatened. The threat that such trends pose to the future of society cannot be overstated. It is this kind of chaos which, according to Pierre Bertaux, produces 'human mutations'—"the rotten fruit of the social conditions in which they grew." And this uncertainty makes the mission and approach of *The Village Way* more urgent and relevant than ever.

Our educational environment should reflect our greatest hopes for society; it should be our utopia, but sadly, as Neil Postman noted:

"education gave up on utopia." Earlier, it was Rabbi Abraham Joshua Heschel who lamented about the absence of the sublime from education. Indeed, *The Village Way* regards the educational environment as a "miniature nation"—a utopia in a nutshell –in which educators assume the role of "nation builders" whose role is to reinstate the utopian dimension of education. *The Village Way* is the practical embodiment of this utopian vision.

Over the last decade, scholars from various disciplines have begun to admit that the profusion of theories, disciplines and trends *by itself* perpetuates and adds to the existing chaos. This observation is relevant to the field of education, in which a flood of programs and guidelines flows uninterruptedly. Educators themselves need to return to the essential elements of their practice and understanding to provide these foundations.

The Village Way is about simplicity. Educators and children value an ongoing process in which all participants grow, learn, and become whole together. Yet in this simplicity, it offers a solution to some of the most pressing issues of our time. *The Village Way* takes theories and connects them to the practical reality of the global village. The role of educators as nation builders is essential, as evidenced in those countries where teachers are most highly prized, such as Finland and South Korea. Not surprisingly, those nations now rank at the top of international appraisal of scholastic achievements.

Adolescence for at-risk youth is a painfully brief and transient hour of grace. First we must counteract the destructiveness of their early upbringing. Then we must show them what is possible. All of these endeavors must be done within the context of their own culture, their homeland. The *Village Way* provides the practical, the ideological, and the possible. And not just for the child. For the educator, *The Village Way* presents these three components as well with the opportunity to affect the broader landscape, well beyond our specific village to the collection of villages that we build in service to the nation.

ADOLESCENCE:
AN HOUR OF GRACE

This book is the story of a powerful belief in adolescence as an hour of grace. Not another "how to" guide—but a source of transformational insight into the reader's relationships with teenagers. By sharing my life experience, I hope to re-ignite in my readers the will, ability and confidence to become our teenagers' guides and mentors.

My experience is grounded in the Yemin Orde Wingate Youth Village in Israel, a residential educational community where I served as director and head educator for nearly 30 years, and whose pulse of life provides the inspiration for this book. Yemin Orde, as it is known, grew out of a need to provide a focal point for young souls wandering in the aftermath of historical ruptures and devastation, left void of parental guidance. Founded in 1953 in the fledgling state of Israel, the village is named in honor of Orde Charles Wingate, the British Brigadier General who helped establish the State of Israel. Since its inception, this 77-acre village on Mt. Carmel, which is just south of Haifa, has provided refuge to waves of children who have come to Israel in the aftermath of the convulsive upheavals of recent history. In this regard, the village, which houses hundreds of children, is a microcosm for the State of Israel itself: our children have come to us from the former Soviet Union, from Ethiopia, from South America and even from Darfur—among other locales. Most of the thousands of children and teenagers who arrived at this haven have experienced painful separations; their lives marred by heartbreaking family situations that left them confused and frustrated. These teenagers have been and remain my greatest teachers.

Some readers may ask, justifiably, whether lessons learned from teenagers coming from such extreme circumstances apply to the children they encounter. I am convinced that the answer is yes. Contemporary conditions dictate that even in the most "normal" of homes, adult presence has been weakened, thus opening a void that is being filled with artificial substitutes for the real thing. The real thing, of course, is in those who gave life to the children; where that is unavailable, as at Yemin Orde, it also resides in those who feel responsible for them.

But it is not merely an adult presence that can make a difference in adolescent lives—it is the quality of that presence. This is true no matter how privileged or how challenged these lives have been. For despite the prevalence of teenage rebellion and its implied rejection of adult guidance, our youngsters want and need our presence. What I have learned at Yemin Orde is that even in the most unfavorable of circumstances we can raise children within an atmosphere of parental wholeness and offer them a bridge to a healthy and dynamic adulthood. I believe that if we can do it here, you can do it with your children and students, just about anywhere you may be.

Despite all of the difficulties and challenges inherent in educating teenagers, these years in fact represent a highly favorable moment for educators. Among the many energies bursting forth from our children during adolescence are extraordinary powers for healing past traumas and the scars they have left behind. As educators, we must not view these years as a black hole in which only minor changes are possible in youngsters whose personalities have already been fixed and sealed. On the contrary, adolescence is a period during which powerful forces are constantly at work that bring about a revolution in our adolescents' psyches.

Before I go on, let me take a moment to explain my approach in writing this book. This work is an effort to aid educators as they guide adolescents toward lives that are meaningful and complete. For clarity's sake, I will articulate my views in sections, each addressing a component of the approach. Still, what I am advocating here is a holistic method of education, the components of which must be understood first and foremost to exist not in a vacuum, but each in relation to the others. Every one of the parts must, therefore, reflect the totality and give it meaning. Holism refers to a conception of life as a harmonious totality in which one thing is woven into the next. Just as holistic medicine aims to treat the entire person—not merely a limb, or an illness, or an individual symptom—this educational approach strives to address the totality of the human being. In such a conception, it is sometimes difficult to distinguish between the forest and the trees—not only is the totality composed of details, but every detail encompasses within it the entirety of the story.

THE SECRET OF BEING A HUMAN BEING

In contemporary society, many educators (not to mention parents) suffer from a lack of confidence in their ability to guide children through the crucial years when they are becoming adults. Young people often angrily reject their elders' authority, values and ideals—or else sink into depression, anxiety or a slow-burning and passive hostility. Educators often feel frustrated, angry or wounded by what they perceive as teenagers' disdain and impudence, or else feel a gnawing anxiety about their charges' lack of passion, vitality and initiative. This anxiety has bred entire industries over recent decades—notably the tough-love military-style schools and summer camps, whose goal is to almost violently break down rebellious teenagers' resistance to adult discipline.

The crisis of confidence regarding adolescents that challenges many educators today is the result of the unraveling of traditional structures of meaning and community that have existed for thousands of years. Modern psychological theories, whose ideas have successfully penetrated our general culture, see human beings as motivated by instinctual drives, such as the sexual drive, or by the ego's desire for autonomy and control. Although these drives and desires certainly exist, they offer at best a fragmentary view of what people really want. Human beings are first and foremost creatures that seek not sexual release or control and autonomy—however crucial these are—but human contact and the unfolding and realization of the fullness of their individual identity within the tapestry of social life. The human psyche is hard-wired to find meaning in an existential context dense with interaction and cooperation between generations. Whether they know it consciously or not, children expect the generation that brought them into the world to transmit to them the secret of what it means to be a human being. When teenagers intuitively feel that they are not receiving this knowledge, which cannot be conveyed through words alone but must be passed on by living example, they respond with inner disorder expressed in frustration, rebellion and anger.

The task of providing young people with the kind of example they seek sounds daunting, nearly impossible. The good news this book brings is that as educators, we can, through certain simple but immensely significant shifts of attitude and intent, provide children with the taste and aura of wholeness and meaning that they so deeply need.

Indeed, educators must always see both themselves and the person standing in front of them—broken as they all may be—as complete human beings. We must always remain cognizant that our primary task is to foster an environment in which this completeness can achieve its fullest expression. This approach echoes a chain of thought that begins with the author of Psalms, continues with Rabbi Nachman of Breslov via John Dewey and Kurt Hahn, and culminates with Martin Buber. This list isn't exhaustive, but it is sufficient to highlight the connecting thread. Our goal is not to create for our charges some super-human reality that is perfect and final. What we're talking about here is simply the effort to create an environment that allows our adolescents to fully experience life—both what is visible and what is hidden, the quotidian and the sublime. In this way, we can hope to expand the boundaries of how they, and we, observe and experience reality, and thus enrich the ways in which they, and we, interpret this reality and act within it.

Once upon a time, the centrality of the relationship between parents and children could be taken for granted. When most of humanity lived in villages and tribal communities, surrounded by their extended families, a sense of coherence and meaning was woven into the natural flow of life. Children grew and developed within the atmosphere of parental wholeness—meaning that parents, alongside teachers and other significant adult figures, radiated an emotionally coherent set of qualities, connections and values that anchored children within the human world of which they were becoming part.

The transformation of adolescence into a time sharply marked by intergenerational conflict coincides with the post-industrial era in the Western world, in which "the village" and all the communal values it embodies has been replaced by the predominance of urban life and the isolated nuclear family. That this reality should lead to a continuous cycle of irreconcilable rifts between generations is not something we need to accept as an immutable decree. Returning to the roots of human nature, in which children are raised within an aura of parental wholeness, is still a choice we can make, as the stories and the thoughts in the coming pages will demonstrate.

Over the years at Yemin Orde we have discovered that the possibility of offering parental wholeness to our children—within the circumstances implied by modern living, and despite the fact that their biological parents are no longer in the picture—is not dependent on accumulating stores of knowledge or pedagogical techniques per se, but on an inner state of mind that affects the way we view the task of educating and parenting. Folded up within the term "parental wholeness" is the belief that, although educators can never truly replace biological parents, a concerted effort, coupled with great stores of sensitivity on their part, will allow educators to at least *represent* the parental wholeness that every adolescent deserves. This aspiration led us to search for an apparatus that could help activate that missing quality of parental presence in our adolescents. We believe we have found one.

MENDING THE WORLD—MENDING THE HEART

Within the tumultuous reality in which we educate our children, locating and identifying the inner point of gravity from which we can radiate wholeness is essential. The central message I wish to convey to you is that greatness in education can be achieved through a fundamental shift in awareness. To make this shift as educators, we can refer to very simple symbols. Specifically, two circles and two lines. These symbols, when absorbed into one's consciousness, will become an almost instinctive point of reference—our inner point of gravity.

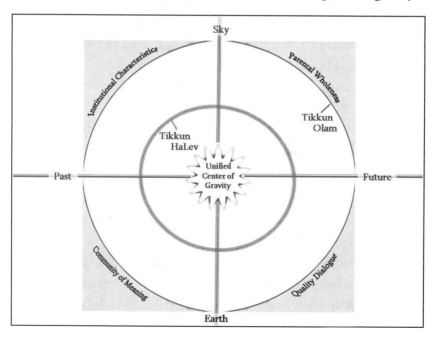

One of the two lines represents the flow of time, moving horizontally from the past to the future. The other line runs vertically, from the gritty, physical and emotional reality of the present moment, which we will call "earth," upwards towards timeless spiritual and ethical values, which we will call "sky."

The two circles are concentric: one inside the other, like the circles drawn on a target. The outer circle we call the circle of *Tikkun Olam*, or mending of the world. The inner circle we call *Tikkun HaLev*, or mending of the heart. These two terms are borrowed from the *Kabbalah*, the Jewish mystical tradition. In the kabbalistic tradition, the human heart is seen as a microcosm of the entire universe. The great world outside and the inner world of emotions and identity are intimately related to each other. Only by understanding and attempting to shape and repair the larger world in which we live can we find the insight and strength to fix our inner world. At the same time, without becoming aware of our inner world and the process and possibility of emotional healing, our attempts to focus on the world at large will be handicapped.

Consciously embracing our role as educators can aid us in discovering, amidst all the seemingly broken pieces of our own existence, an inner unity of intention located where the center of the lines and circles meet. This unity, when children become aware of it, enables them to perceive us as mentors in a deep sense. The lines are the coordinates that trace both our adolescents' internal worlds and our own, while the circles encompass the space that we share with them, and in which mentoring happens.

The significance of these lines and circles will become clearer as the book progresses, and they will, I hope, develop into a ready frame of reference. As educators, an awareness of this framework will allow us to transform the various situations and conflicts that lie ahead in our relationships with our charges into a new realm touched by the aura of wholeness. And we also can regard this framework as a symbolic matrix within which we can find our own center of gravity, and offer the children in our care the nearest equivalent to parental presence.

MENTORING: A VILLAGE STATE OF MIND

A common mark of confident adults is the decisive influence, during their formative years, of a mentor. If we have had such an influence, we are well aware of the difference it has made in our life. The mentor's impact is felt as much through his or her attention and presence as through the specific content of what he or she gives us. Seemingly, the task of mentoring should be suited only for those adults who have got "it"—who have the requisite charisma, stamina and conviction to produce the mentoring effect. True, every young person deserves a worthy mentor; it is my conviction that all reasonably sound adults have the mentoring spirit within themselves, if they know where to search.

Mentoring, I believe, begins with reconstructing the outline of the lost village of humankind within ourselves. The famous African proverb "It takes a village to raise a child," which Hillary Rodham Clinton reintroduced into the American consciousness, reverberates with humankind's longing for this lost village. But we cannot return to the lost village. What we have the privilege of doing is using our awareness and insight to recreate, starting within ourselves, the "village state of mind"—reproducing, through our own free choice and intention, the sense of connection with others that is part of the structure of human consciousness.

Our vision at Yemin Orde has been to ensure that behind each child is an educational community designed to reproduce the basic outline of humanity's lost village—a village that can instill in its children a recognition and pride in their past, a sense of direction and security about the future, an openness to transcendent values, a desire to improve communal reality, and a deeper understanding and insight of their weaknesses and strengths.

Teenagers certainly cannot do this without a sense of support and community. We need to offer them an aura of togetherness, a sense of inner coherence and emotional solidarity that defies the swirling chaos surrounding us. We must recreate, intentionally, through the messages that we constantly broadcast to our children, the sense of belonging and togetherness that once defined human existence.

Is reconstructing the lost village within us an unrealizable task? Absolutely not. For our many graduates, reconstructing the village in their own hearts has proved possible. Indeed, it is observing these graduates, many now successful parents and mentors themselves, that has convinced me that the principles we have discovered and put into action at Yemin Orde are relevant and replicable elsewhere.

What is left now is to share with you the essence of our experience, its foundations and its practical implications. I invite you to follow our story and find personal meaning in the human task of mentoring, thus inspiring a new generation capable of transforming the global village by infusing it with the contours and qualities of the original human village.

FRAGMENTS OF PARENTING, SLIVERS OF LOVE

2

My own childhood begins during the tragic years of World War II and has a devastating absence at its center. I mention this because I believe that the energies and attitudes we bring to our work as educators (not to mention as parents) have their origins in our own childhoods. The deciphering of our childhood and teenage experiences is a central component of our inner lives no matter what stage of life we have reached.

My mother came to Israel, then ruled by the British, in the late 1930s at the age of 17. Her family had immigrated to Hanover, Germany in order to escape the grinding poverty and anti-Semitism of the Polish shtetl. Most of the Jews of Poland, including my mother's family, were Hasidim, devout followers of a mystical form of Judaism that emphasized community, ecstatic devotion, and strict observance. In Germany, Jewish immigrants from Poland were considered primitive by their more modern and secularized German Jewish counterparts. As immigrants without German citizenship or a supportive social network, they were especially vulnerable to Nazism.

The Nazis had already taken power and were beginning to reveal their cruel talons when my mother left Germany, although few yet guessed the extent of the murderous depravity they intended. From the moment of her arrival in Palestine, my mother attempted to obtain entry permits, called "certificates," so that her parents and younger brother could join her in the Land of Israel. She stood in lines for countless hours, trying to navigate the Byzantine bureaucracy of the British, whose main concern was to prevent the mass immigration of Jews into the country. To support herself, my mother worked picking oranges, cleaning houses, and caring for small children. She met my father, an electrical engineer with his own saga of family separation and tragedy, and married him in 1940.

Soon she was pregnant with me. During the entire course of her pregnancy, my mother continued to work cleaning houses, and in her spare time redoubled her efforts to rescue her family. By now, the Germans had expelled them to a refugee camp on the Polish border. She received a last postcard from them that I still have. In it her father complains about her little brother, who in the crowded camp has stopped studying Torah—the traditional term for the Bible and other religious texts that Jews are commanded to "meditate on morning and night." Instead, her father writes, her brother has fashioned a ball for himself out of rags, and plays games with it in the dirty alleys of the camp.

Near the end of her pregnancy, my mother became ill with typhoid, and was weak when she gave birth to me in September of 1941. After learning that her parents and brother had been murdered by the Nazi machine, and that all her efforts to save them had ended in failure, she suffered a mental breakdown and was admitted to a mental hospital. She eventually was released, but my mother was never the same. She lived the rest of her life alternating between mostly unsuccessful attempts to live a normal life at home and periods of confinement in mental institutions.

In light of these circumstances, my father, who was unable to raise me alone, placed me as a baby in an institution for homeless children in Tel Aviv. I stayed there until I myself almost died of typhoid at the age of two. My grandmother rescued me from this institution, and I lived with her off and on until I was six or seven, when I returned to my father and mother. They had divorced when I was four, but had reunited a year later. Although my father was only a distant presence as a parent, too ensconced in his own thoughts and involved with his own life struggles to reach out emotionally to me, I have always admired the courage and integrity of his choice. Despite my mother's suffering, depression and instability, he chose to live with her rather than abandon her.

My father fought in the 1948 War of Independence and took part in the Jewish conquest of Acre, an ancient seaport in northern Israel that filled up after the war with new Jewish immigrants, many of them Holocaust survivors. My father moved us there. One of the notable architectural features of Acre was a medieval castle located in the old city, which the British had used as a jail for political prisoners; some of the captured heroes of the Jewish resistance had been hanged there. The castle, which was surrounded by a moat that once was filled with seawater, had been taken over by the new Israeli government and given to the Ministry of Health for use as an insane asylum. The castle-turned-prison-turned-asylum was located right across the street from my school. As a child, I remember seeing the castle through the window of my classroom, knowing my mother was interned inside. The high castle walls and the impassable moat symbolized for me the impossibility that I would ever have a normal childhood or a stable home.

Between periods in the asylum, my mother often was melancholy. When her depression turned psychotic, I sometimes would have to chase my half-dressed mother through the streets of town. I remember, at least once, bringing her myself to the asylum, where she was put into a room filled with other mentally ill people—men and women, Arabs and Jews. The asylum staff tended to treat the families as if they were extensions of the patients themselves. I felt as if the staff, the doctors, the very wards of the institution itself were trying to suck me into their midst, where I would disappear forever.

THE ABSENT PARENT SYNDROME

A mentally ill parent is for me the ultimate symbol of the kind of parent that the novelist Ian McEwan has found symptomatic of the 20th century—not fully present even when physically close. And yet my experience with my mother also taught me that fragments of good parenting, of love—which in many ways are the basis of good educating—are absorbed by children and later can be built into structures that lead to wholeness. Even in the insanity of the household in which I was raised, I had some sort of compass. In her brief periods free of psychosis or depression, my mother would intermittently show me samples of what true love meant. These were outbursts of normalcy that I could grasp, and it is impossible to exaggerate their importance. As I later learned in my work as an educator, children can build whole worlds out of such slivers of parental love.

Still, it took me years to deal with my childhood, to make peace with it. It was a childhood in which I lacked any model of parental wholeness. I could see only brokenness. And yet this shattering, this hole where the center should have been, sharpened my intuition; the very absence of parental wholeness in my life gave me a sense, one might say, of what it ought to smell like, and has thus guided the development of my educational thinking.

THE ABSOLUTE FORMATIVE POWER OF ADOLESCENCE

I began to recover from my childhood during my teenage years, through exposure to healthy parental figures and family environments that radiated wholeness—environments I was attracted to as a moth is to light. This experience planted within me the seeds of two important convictions.

The first is my belief in the absolutely formative power of adolescence, no matter what was one's experience of childhood. One of Freud's important insights, among the most influential ideas of the 20th century, is his emphasis on the crucial impact of the early years of childhood on people's emotional development. Swayed by Freud, educators such as A. S. Neill, founder of the Summerhill School and one of the spiritual fathers of the experimental and democratic school movement, believed that a child's psychological makeup could not be radically altered after the age of seven or eight.

Without diminishing the significance of the early childhood years, the conviction that the teenage years are equally momentous in their shaping power has been the beacon of my educational approach. Although the seeds of this conviction were sown through my own experience growing up, I have had this belief confirmed time and time again during my years of working with teenagers who were able, during adolescence, to heal childhood traumas and change the trajectory of their lives. If I could tell every educator just one thing, it would be that each hour of the teenage years is precious, each experience as potent in its capability to heal or to wound as countless hours of childhood experiences.

Many boarding schools, orphanages and therapeutic centers have become preoccupied with digging into children's wounds—and this emphasis is reflected in how their caretakers carry out their work. But all of the treatment this approach entails takes up just a small fraction of any 24-hour day. The remaining hours are simply comprised of child warehousing. This approach misses out on innumerable opportunities to build and reinforce a sense of structure and cohesion in the lives of these children, who for so long have lacked it. We cannot forget that children who have been abandoned once (or more than once) often believe that the future is sure to hold another traumatic dislocation. As this mindset takes hold, these children are likely to hold on also to the detrimental behaviors and skills that go along with it. If they needed the skills to survive yesterday, their thinking goes, they will need them tomorrow as well. But to that we at Yemin Orde say, *No! The cycle of being dumped is over. What happened in the past is in the past. It will not happen again in the future.* Our approach calls for instilling in these children a larger sense of structure—a structure in which therapy finds a place but is not the beginning, middle and end. The message that the adolescent will not be abandoned again must not only be spoken, but experienced. This fundamental position is very different from the approach that views education as the transmission of life skills. What I am advocating here is something much deeper than helping teenagers acquire tools and skills—indeed, our village strives to strengthen the psyches of its youth, not their functionality. This is achieved by introducing into the children's awareness the six elements on the two-lines and two-circles continuum. When they reach us, these children's societies are falling apart. If we wish to transform them before sending them back out in to the world, their time with us must be marked by a sense of structure and cohesion, and the promise of a long-term commitment to their well-being.

PARENTAL PRESENCE—
BUILDING UP A WHOLESOME PERSONALITY

The second belief I bring with me from my adolescence is that parental figures (be they the biological parents or educators acting in their stead) are no less crucial to teenagers than they are to infants, although in a different way. We know that infants need constant care. Although it is less obvious, this is equally true for adolescents. This truth is easy to miss, since a struggle to be independent and an urge to rebel also characterize the teenage years. But adolescents need a very specific kind of parental presence. Their overarching need is for us to radiate an aura of wholeness amidst the chaos they experience both in the world and within their own fragmented psyches—a chaos they often embody and express in outbursts directed at authority figures. Offering adolescents this kind of support may seem an amorphous and impenetrable task, but, as I hope to show, it is indeed an attainable goal.

One way to reflect on these insights—the formative nature of adolescence and the adolescent's thirst for her parents' presence in her life—is to recognize that we bear responsibility for our children's future memories. Our inner life continues to be profoundly connected to our experiences in childhood and adolescence for as long as we live. For much of the rest of our lives, we are engaged in remembering and deciphering our early years, which adolescence crowns and seals. Our relationship with our children can thus be seen as a seeding for the future.

Looking back on our childhood and adolescence, we tend to think that our psyches were deeply influenced by dramatic or extraordinary events. But in the end, it is the mundane and the everyday that are engrained in us, forming the emotional and cognitive patterns of our personalities. I have often thought about how different the narratives of countless children's lives would be if their educators and parents had acted with the awareness that they were writing, day by day, the memories that would stay with these children forever.

At times, while attending weddings or other joyous events of our alumni, shreds of memory, images from their adolescence, cross my mind—memories that run in sharp contrast to the uplifting occasion. Whenever this happens, I re-experience the sometimes horrendous incidents of the past. Strangely enough, at times like these I am overwhelmed by a triumphant sense of the incredible healing power of adolescence. It is my hope that you eventually will experience a similar sense of triumph, at the end of the lengthy path you will travel with the adolescents who are part of your life. This book is a first step on this journey.

3

EDUCATIONAL ENVIRONMENTS THAT SPEAK WHOLENESS

Founded soon after the birth of the State of Israel, Yemin Orde Youth Village, like Israel itself, has been a crucible in which children from North Africa, the Near East, Europe, South America, and later on from tiny Ethiopian villages far removed from Western civilization, have found themselves living alongside each other. Teens whose childhoods were marred by traumas and who have wounds of almost indescribable severity have struggled, rebelled, and finally flourished alongside children of backgrounds-from within Israel.

Yemin Orde is situated on 77 acres on a western slope of the Carmel Mountain range overlooking the Mediterranean Sea near Haifa, Israel's third largest city. Below our Village is scenic Ein Hod, a famous artists' colony. If you were to look at Yemin Orde from a birds-eye view, you would see a forest of pines, with cypress and cedar trees dotting its periphery and a series of low-slung white buildings with red tile roofs. Along with cottages where 30 staff families live, there are classrooms, a synagogue, a glass-walled dining hall, a modern art center, a small library, two computer centers, twenty children's homes

housing 500 children, and assorted other structures. The campus itself, although surrounded by a fence for security reasons, can be easily breached by teenagers, who often are talented escape artists.

Indeed, one of the first questions that some of the many visitors
to Yemin Orde ask is whether I have trouble with children attempting to "escape" the village, i.e. going AWOL. After all, Haifa and its
malls are nearby, and the beach is so tantalizingly close that it can
be seen from the western edge of the campus. With 500 children in
residence at any given time, one might expect a certain percentage
to desert.

On the whole, however, this does not happen. Although rebellion, protest and other forms of anger directed at authority are a regular and expected part of teenage development here, running away
is not. This is not because our village is a teenager's idea of paradise.
Rather, teenagers remain inside Yemin Orde because they sense that
the adults sharing their lives convey a sense of purpose—a roadmap
that can guide them forward. In accordance with current trends, the
absence of this kind of roadmap in adolescence often invites a search
for answers through various therapies and psychological theories. I
maintain that this search often generates the sickness for which it
purports to be the cure; it replaces the most simple and basic teenage need: to feel solid ground beneath their feet and to see a horizon
of possibilities stretching out in front of them—both for themselves
and for the world their generation will inherit.

That is because the connection between the "treater" and the
"treatee" is inherently asymmetrical. The therapist, by definition
and by training, must divest himself of aspects of his personality in
order to focus on his task, which is based in scientific knowledge.
In the course of his training the therapist acquires the fundamentals
of this knowledge—and over the course of his career, keeps himself continuously updated on the field's development. The body of
knowledge that accumulates is generalizing in its nature. It does not

deal with phenomena unique to this or that patient, but with general trends. Further, it is not the therapist's job to enter into a dialogue with the patient. Rather, his function in the division of labor is simply to represent therapeutic expertise.

It is as such that educators should not function as therapists. If therapeutic relationships were to take the lead in education, this would dehumanize the adolescents we are seeking to make into complete humans. We must therefore be careful to preserve the distinction between the educational reality and the therapeutic task.

HIDDEN SOURCES OF STRENGTH

Being an educator means, first and foremost, learning from your students all the time. In my case, it has afforded me the chance to learn from many kinds of stories and experiences of adolescence, emanating from vastly different locations and cultures. Perhaps none has affected me as deeply as the story of the Ethiopian-Jewish youngsters who began to arrive at Yemin Orde beginning in the fall of 1981. Contemplating these youngsters and their hidden sources of strength reawakened and reinforced the lessons I had learned in my own childhood about the resilience of adolescence and the thirst for the guiding presence of a mentor.

The first Ethiopian teenagers who arrived at Yemin Orde in 1981 were newcomers not only to the village, but also to Israel itself. They were part of the first trickle of what would become, over the next decade, a wave of new immigrants from war-torn Ethiopia, and they composed the first mass immigration of a Jewish tribe from East Africa to Israel. This immigration confronted us with a virtually unprecedented phenomenon in the history of mankind: the nearly instantaneous migration of an entire community—whose way of life had not changed for thousands of years—to a hyper-modern state where they arrived as full citizens.

The Ethiopians stood out from the other teenagers in the village by virtue of their skin color—and because they were heirs to an ancient Jewish tradition with its own unique customs and religious interpretations that differed from every other Jewish community in the world. But what was extraordinary to me about these youngsters was not their color, nor even their fascinating traditions. It was the route that they had taken to reach Israel. Despite constant peril to their lives, most of these youngsters had walked hundreds of miles through bandit-infested mountains and deserts to make it out of Communist Ethiopia and into Sudan, where a route to the Promised Land had tenuously and perilously opened up.

Traveling in groups where teenagers often outnumbered adults, these youngsters had braved hunger, thirst, disease, outlaws, wild animals, and the fury of government soldiers who considered their exodus a betrayal. At some point during the exodus, virtually all of these young people had witnessed the deaths of close relatives, including siblings, parents and grandparents. Often, they themselves had nearly died of starvation, illness or external threat.

And yet, though the traumas they experienced remained etched in their memories, these young people mainly recalled the exuberance and stamina that had lifted them across the wilderness, as if they were ships whose sails had been filled by their own mighty spirits. I knew that if I could find a way to help them tap into that amazing spirit again, it could propel them across the next chasm they would have to navigate. Within a period of months, they would have to speed along a path that had taken a much of civilization hundreds of years to cross.

INNER ROADMAP

Where in fact were these teenagers coming from if not from the lost village of humanity, which had survived in Ethiopia, the cradle of human civilization, into the 21st century? It was the rural African village—familial and enveloping, operating on a social structure that had capably sustained and transmitted its values to generation after generation of its children—that was the source of their strength. However, while we in the West lost this village mentality over the course of the last several hundred years, these young Ethiopian Jews stood to lose it nearly instantly in their transition to the new world of mass culture and alienating Western cities. I would learn, however, that the values and sustenance that had been transmitted to them by the village can be retained by the human heart long after geographical and historical borders are left behind.

Eighteen years later, in the winter of 1999, I found myself reflecting again on the astonishingly resourceful spirit concealed in seemingly average adolescents. I was in Chuntra, a children's village in a region of northern India where hundreds of children and adolescent refugees from Chinese-occupied Tibet had found a new home. I had traveled to India as part of a continuing dialogue with Tibetan educators that would eventually bring Tibetan youngsters to Israel to study at Yemin Orde. Many of the refugees in Chuntra were children who had fled a world shattered by the Chinese assault on Tibetan cultural and religious life. In order to find a new life, they were forced to uproot themselves from their friends and family.

As I listened to these young Tibetans tell their stories, the ordeals they had endured came alive in my imagination. I could picture them making their way by foot through treacherous mountain passes. I could see the fear in their young faces as they thought they heard the voices of a Chinese army patrol approaching them from around a bend, and their joy and relief when such fears proved unfounded. I could see them building a campfire in the cold night air, eating a meager meal with a sense of gratitude for whatever they had managed to find. I could almost taste their tears, as they lay wrapped in their blankets, thinking about the family they had left behind and might never see again. I could also imagine the excitement on their faces as they crossed into India on their way to the new life for which they had sacrificed so much.

As I sat in the shadow of the Himalayan Mountains, the unfamiliar smell of Tibetan cooking spices wafting in from another room, I was reminded of the Ethiopian children whose path through a different kind of wilderness was really so similar. Like the Tibetans, they had endured a terrible ordeal. What was even more powerful than the conjunction of external circumstances was the interior similarities between the Ethiopian Jewish and Tibetan teenagers. Both had displayed enormous resilience and vitality in the face of danger, hardship, and the threat of death. Like migratory birds on their epoch flights across continents, traversing deserts and mighty mountain peaks, these teenagers had been able to marshal all their powers in a nearly superhuman effort.

From where had they drawn this strength? It seemed obvious that it was their clarity of purpose that gave them so much inner power. I could detect a tremendous drive toward life in the Tibetan and Ethiopian children, a zest for the possibilities offered by the new kind of existence that lay just over the ridge, past the next snowdrift, or just beyond the border. The Tibetan teenagers, too, stood to lose the web of meaning that had nourished them during their childhood—the fast-disappearing traditional human village. Yet perhaps this "village state of mind," cultivated over so many thousands of years and hundreds of generations, lives inside each of us as a potential awaiting activation?

On the face of it, the strength and vitality of the Ethiopian and Tibetan children would seem to have had little to do with parental presence. After all, many of the Ethiopian and Tibetan teens whose stories amazed me did not have parents with them on their arduous journeys. Yet a feeling of being guided by the generation that brought them into the world is something children absorb so deeply that it transcends physical presence. Children and teenagers can draw from the aura of parental presence no matter where they are. Both groups of teenagers drew their strength from the knowledge that in attempting their journey, they were fulfilling the deepest dreams and aspirations of their ancestors. These dreams functioned like an inner roadmap. They marked the final destination of the journey in bold colors, and fixed within the psyche of each child his personal connection to the journey.

To grow up in an Ethiopian Jewish village—where every older person was empowered with parental authority and charged with a parental role in relation to the village's children—meant being exposed every single day to the communal dream of returning to Jerusalem. "If we did a good deed, or fulfilled a task well, an elder might say to us, 'I bless you to return to our land,' meaning Zion, Jerusalem," says Negiste, who was 14 years old when she set out for Sudan. The journey to Jerusalem, via Sudan, was thus an adventure into the unknown shielded, supported, and inspired by values that the children had absorbed into their own identities since birth.

The Tibetan children also came from a community in which mundane events and interactions with parents and elders served as a loom on which ancient traditions and future hopes were woven daily into a tapestry of meaning. The flight from Chinese-occupied Tibet was a flight to the Dalai Lama in exile in India and the autonomous Tibetan culture he represented. The incalculable value of this culture was an axiom, part of the air that surrounded the children as they moved through the village environment, an axiom that was the covert subtext of all their encounters with parents, teachers and elders.

These groups of African and Asian adolescents thus moved through a world that had been given to them by an older generation who had collectively raised them since the moment of their birth. It was a world whose meaning and direction were mediated by tangible authority figures. The convictions and values of the elders passed over to the children on a bridge built by the relationship between the generations. The youngsters moving through deserts, jungles and snowy mountain passes might have appeared as if they were alone, but they were not. They carried the imprint of their parents' spirit inside of them.

It seemed to me that reconstituting that spirit and allowing parental guidance to hold a central place within the relationship between generations (even if the biological parents were no longer in the picture) would bring us a long way toward reclaiming our birthright—the lost village of humanity.

SHALOM: THE SPIRITUAL IMPRINT OF PARENTS

For years, I have pondered the power of parents to continue to inspire their children long after their power and authority—or even their lives—have waned.

This power is essential, I believe, because in our constantly developing and changing society, all our children are destined to live in a world substantially different from our own. The story of Shalom, one of the children raised at Yemin Orde who is now himself an educator with hundreds of children in his charge, illustrates this.

Shalom was the youngest in his family, his mother having died while giving birth to him. He was only nine years old when he crossed the deserts and mountains on the way to Sudan. His father, already an older man, was also along on this journey, although some of his older sisters and brothers had stayed behind. His grandmother, whom he remembered as a woman of great piety and virtue, had died shortly before the family left. She had prophesized correctly that she would not make it to Israel alive, but that her children and grandchildren would.

Shalom's father struggled to keep the family alive on the journey. In the Sudanese refugee camps, as the Jews awaited planes that would take them to Israel, many fell victim to diseases that raced through the weakened population. Jewish custom dictates that burial take place on the day of death, but this was perilous because the burials also had to be carried out secretly. If the other refugees knew that there were Jews in their midst, a dangerous situation would have ensued. Shalom's father risked his life time and again in order to bring his friends and relatives to burial in the traditional manner. All throughout this period, Shalom saw his father as a hero: strong, courageous, and self-sacrificing.

Once in Israel, though, Shalom's father was like a fish out of water. It was difficult for him to adjust to the strange customs of the new land. In the first few months following their arrival, the Ethiopian immigrants were housed in hotels that served as temporary absorption centers. "They would bring us plates of beef or chicken, but my father and some of the other elders wouldn't eat it," Shalom tells me. They felt uncomfortable eating in a massive dining hall, with the food placed on the table for everyone to grab. At home, they were the ones to distribute the portions of food, in a ritual that reinforced their status. Here, everyone served himself or herself, without consideration of hierarchy or custom.

Shalom's father never found work in Israel, and in a somatic expression of his inability to fully adjust to his new life, developed chronic asthma. "He was an extremely talented man, but here in this new situation, he just sat around and did nothing," Shalom says. But Shalom's admiration for him did not abate. "I used to walk hand in hand with him to synagogue on Saturday morning. I felt that as long as we were together we were surrounded with an aura, a kind of halo of light."

Shalom was attending school some distance away when he felt a compulsion to return home for the weekend. When he arrived, he learned that his father was in the hospital. "I stayed by his bedside the next 24 hours, as he fell in and out of consciousness," Shalom says. "Early that morning, he passed away."

Shalom, who was entering the 9th grade, was sent to our village soon after his father's death. It was difficult for him to concentrate. He was obsessed with thoughts of death and, at times, especially when thinking about his father, he would sink into an almost hypnotic trance from which he could be roused only by a loud shout or even a pinch.

One day in late May 1991, Shalom was at home for the weekend when he saw a television broadcast announcing the successful conclusion of Operation Solomon, an airlift in which the 14,500 Jews remaining in Ethiopia—including, presumably, Shalom's older sisters and brothers—had been flown to Israel. The airlift, which had taken only 26 hours, had been kept secret until its completion. Shalom immediately set out to find his long-lost family, hitching a ride to the city of Tiberias where some of the immigrants had been temporarily settled. After a nearly miraculous series of coincidences, Shalom located one of his sisters, whom he had not seen in seven years. Along with her husband and seven children, she was housed in a hotel, much as Shalom and his father had been when they first arrived.

In the excitement of the moment, Shalom forgot to inform us at Yemin Orde of his whereabouts. Instead, he offered his services as a translator to the Israeli staff members who were trying as best as they could to see to the basic needs of the new immigrants, but feeling justifiably overwhelmed by their task. For the first time, Shalom felt that he had the opportunity to fill the shoes of his father who had risked everything to help family and friends during the journey to Sudan and in the refugee camps. There was the feeling of completing a circle; while his father had been made helpless in the new reality of the absorption-center hotels, Shalom was now adept at both the Hebrew language and Israeli customs. Shalom spent the next two weeks helping the immigrants and the staff understand each other, and when he left, he was awarded a testimonial plaque thanking him for his enormous contribution.

Shalom expected to be disciplined by Yemin Orde for having disappeared for two weeks. Instead, when we learned where he had been, we greeted him as a returning hero and made a point of placing a copy of his testimonial in his personal file.

From that period on, Shalom's fear diminished, his concentration improved, and he began to excel at his studies. Life had offered him an opportunity to embody the best qualities of his father in a new situation, in some sense healing the experience of bearing witness to his father's weakness during the period immediately following their arrival in Israel. The ghosts of the past were exorcised, allowing Shalom to draw strength from his father's strength once again. Our village's contribution was in the dynamic flexibility that is part and parcel of our approach. Our sensitivity to current events, to personal history and to the ways in which they sometimes intersect, allowed us to understand Shalom's absence not as an inexcusable breach of trust, but as a potentially unique moment of healing, thus legitimating the spiritual imprint that Shalom's parents had left within him.

Restoring the Elixir of Parental Presence

Of course, many of you do not deal regularly with children like these teenage immigrants from Ethiopia and young refugees from Tibet. Still, as I consider their situation, I cannot not help but think about teenagers growing up in the material comfort extant in much of the Western world. What a contrast the two sets of teenagers present—the Ethiopians and Tibetans who were eager to overcome all hardship in the pursuit of a new life, and those growing up in middle or upper class families in Europe, America and elsewhere in the developed world. These are teenagers all of us know—the children of relative abundance, seemingly surrounded by everything they might possibly need, from stereos and computers to video cameras and iPhones. These kids have never had to go to bed hungry or cold, have never felt an immediate threat to their lives. How many of these teenagers in the midst of this abundance are growing up confused, with no real direction in life? How many parents feel they have lost control over their children's lives and, perhaps even more devastatingly, have lost the ability to provide their children with guidance and emotional support? How many parents and children, teachers and students, are caught in a seemingly unending circle of anger and recrimination, disappointment and crushed expectations? What is blocking and stifling the emotional progress of so many well-to-do children? I believe that what we have learned working with adolescents in extreme circumstances can be instructive in helping to overcome many of the challenges we face as educators in approaching children in less extreme, if still difficult, situations.

The bored and troubled middle-class teenagers many of us know and the Ethiopian children trekking through the desert and over mountains are made of the same stuff. For is there really such a thing as a child who has been spoiled, has irretrievably gone bad, is rotten to the core? Everything I have learned in four decades as an educator tells me that the powers and the zest for life easily identifiable in teenagers caught in extreme crisis are hiding beneath the surface in even the most bored and aimless of our young people. The question, though, is how to activate these powers. How are we to inspire the deep engagement with life that we want for our children? Would the same bored and lethargic teenagers suddenly develop tremendous powers of survival if necessity looked them in the eye? This kind of transformation did, in fact, occur with upper class teenagers from wealthy Jewish families who found themselves in dire situations during the Holocaust. But does it take life-threatening circumstances to bring out the motivation and resourcefulness in our teenagers?

Middle or upper class teenagers seem to be surrounded by everything they need. But perhaps something is missing from the picture we have drawn. Something so crucial, so basic, that we take it for granted—although we shouldn't anymore, not in the 21st century. There is something that teenagers need like the air they breathe—despite the overt messages to the contrary that they often send us. It is the presence of parents, or parental figures, in their lives. It is that spiritual imprint that Shalom's father left on him, those ancestral dreams that powered the Ethiopian teens across the desert and the Tibetan adolescents beyond the Himalayas.

Since Yemin Orde is a youth village devoted to residential education, most of the 500 youngsters at our facility have experienced the pain of parental absence or abandonment. We have thus devoted much thought to understanding both the nature of the damage to children inflicted by parental absence, and what parental presence means. Many books and articles have been written about restoring parental authority over children and adolescents. But our emphasis is not on restoring parental authority, but on restoring parental *presence*—that hard-to-define elixir that provides teenagers with a sense of guidance as to how to live and be, and the knowledge that the generation that brought them into the world has not abandoned them.

SAMMY: THE RIGHT TO BE RAISED BY A HUMAN BEING

The need for parental figures is so indelibly a part of the human psyche that children who have grown up with a sense of being deprived of parental presence often spend a lifetime consumed with anger, as if a great injustice has been inflicted on them. Deep down, children feel they deserve to be raised by human beings for whom being a parent is one of the central tasks of their life. Since one can only come into the world through the actions of others, through their very bodies, shouldn't these others be responsible for showing you what life is about? At Yemin Orde, our emphasis is on restoring parental presence, even when there is no biological parent in the picture.

I remember realizing the justice of this demand during one unforgettable incident, in the early 1990s, as a young man stood outside my home and pummeled my roof with stones. Sammy had grown up without a father, and his mother was more or less dysfunctional. One of his counselors in the Village had apparently suspected him of stealing, and Sammy had sought me out throughout that day, in an effort to clear his name. On principle, I try to make myself available to the young people in our Village as much as possible. If I am at a meeting and the secretary is guarding against interruptions, the teenagers know that they have my permission to throw pebbles at the offices' back window as a signal that they need to talk to me urgently. But that day I was at meetings away from the village. Sammy couldn't locate me anywhere. In the evening, at home with my family, I heard tremendous thumping sounds coming from above the ceiling. We jumped up thinking we were under some kind of attack. As it turned out, Sammy was throwing not pebbles, but fist-sized rocks at my roof! Then I heard his voice. "My father abandoned me," he screamed at the top of his lungs. "My mother abandoned me, and now you are abandoning me," he said.

I wanted to go outside and stop Sammy, but reminded myself of one of the axioms of our educational philosophy: that when teenagers act out, the behavior must first and foremost be considered a test for us as educators, and a cry for help. I realized that this was a moment when I could not "do" anything. Sammy's rage was so great that that if I stepped outside, I might have been inviting a rock to my head. I was required to think and to interpret what was happening to me, and to Sammy. One part of me wanted to write this young man off as crazy, as pathological, as abnormal. But I pushed aside that impulse. I tried to understand the inner logic of Sammy's deed. The more I thought about it, the more I was able to see things from his perspective. His anger really was justified. The reality of his life was that he had been virtually abandoned by the generation that brought him into the world. His desire to hold me accountable meant that I had succeeded in becoming a parental figure and thus worthy of punishment. I had become the representative of the older generation, and in that sense, I was responsible. I did deserve stoning. It was not he who was abnormal and pathological; it was the situation and the world into which he had been born.

Eventually, the boom of the rocks landing on my roof ceased rattling our house. Sammy ran off into the woods. I waited for him to approach me, which he eventually did. He expected me to be enraged with his behavior, and when he saw that I wasn't angry with him, he knew that I had understood something of the nature of his pain. From then on, he felt a different kind of trust in me. His extreme action and my response to it raised our bond to another level, exemplifying the principle that, without exception, even the worst crises are opportunities for new beginnings.

Sammy started to heal, although the process took many years. Memories of his parents could still trigger violence. Several years later, when he was out of our high school and doing the mandatory army service that is required of Israeli youths, he was involved in a fistfight outside a movie theatre, which earned him a police record. The fight was sparked when another young man cursed his mother, thus prodding his still open wound.

The story has a happy ending. After the army, Sammy went back to the small town in northern Israel where he had been born. His grandmother, the only member of his family from whom he had experienced love and caring, still lived there. Sammy was determined to make her proud. He decided to become a member of the fire department, with hopes of becoming the best firefighter in the town. There was only one problem: his police record made him an undesirable candidate. Knowing that our Village remains committed to our young people long after they leave, Sammy asked me for help. I ended up going all the way to the President of Israel, who has the power to grant pardons and amnesties, to get his record erased. Some months later, Sammy called me. I could hear tremors of exhilaration in his voice. "I just saved my first lives," he said. There had been a car accident on the highway outside of town, and he had made it to the scene very quickly. He had cut through the door, which had been smashed, and pulled out the two passengers just in time. The car exploded after he had dragged them free. "I'm dedicating this rescue to you," he told me. Stories such as Sammy's teach us how deeply parental absence wounds children, and how these wounds can be healed and the feeling of presence restored.

THE WHOLENESS THAT IS
IN OUR DNA

If I had to think of one phrase that could capture the special emotional pain of the past hundred years of Western civilization, I would say that this has been the century of the absent parent. As far back as 1871, Fyodor Dostoyevsky explored this theme in his novel *The Devils*, whose anti-heroes are young men and women from affluent families who have grown up with a sense of neglect that ultimately leads them to commit acts of terrible violence. Instead of guiding their children toward wellsprings that can fill the inner emptiness in which their "devils" are incubating, the parents in Dostoyevsky's novel shrink away, fearful of their responsibility, and scared of the children themselves.

From Dostoyevsky through Kafka and Joyce, some of the greatest modern writers have dwelled on characters with weak or absent parents—among the most recent being the American writer Jonathan Franzen, whose novel *The Corrections* depicts the grown children of a dysfunctional suburban family abandoning their aging parents as a result of a childhood that left them with no sense of intergenerational connection. I think we can learn as much from these authors' representations of the state of humanity as we can from the testimony of philosophers or psychologists. As I mentioned earlier,

Ian McEwan, the brilliant contemporary British novelist has also portrayed this parental absence as the most hauntingly characteristic malaise of the 20th century. In works such as *Atonement* and *A Child in Time*, parents often are absent even when they are present, just as in real life. The parents in McEwan's novels lack the moral and psychic presence in their children's consciousness that would enable them to protect the children from the dislocations and corruption that are borne on the winds of the 21st century.

The idea of the parent who is absent even when physically present poses a strikingly symmetrical counterpart to the parental figures described in the last chapter, who are present in the hearts of their children even when they are physically absent. That is why the syndrome of the absent parent is about much more than physical absence. My own example of an absent parent may be an extreme one. Most parents are not mentally ill, even though our teenage children may sometimes make us feel as if we are. Yet, the central metaphor of absence is a valid description of much of what is wrong with the relationship between parents and teenage children today. Just as my story—and everybody's story—is set within a historical context, if we are to touch the root problems and challenges of contemporary parenting, we may be helped by becoming aware of the larger story within which our personal stories are taking place.

SEARCH ENGINE SEEKING PARENTAL WHOLENESS

This chapter may seem, at first blush, to relate only to parents, and not to those of us whose life's work involves caring for and educating the children of others. Not so. As we will see in the following chapter, it is essential for educators to recognize the primacy of the parent in a child's psyche, almost regardless of who that parent is. Even if we are forced by the nature of our work to assume some parental duties, we must remain ever cognizant of the fact that in the child's mind, the importance of the biological parent has not been diminished.

Meanwhile, as a general definition, we might say that an absent parent is one who is unable to bring the fullness of his or her personality into the task of parenting. These parents are incapable of conveying a sense of their world in their relationships with their children; their ability to touch these children's inner worlds—the realm bound by the circle of *Tikkun HaLev*—is, therefore, limited. This basic deficit is already the starting point for much teenage frustration and provocation. When parents succeed in conveying to their offspring more than one major dimension of their personality, they also are able to transfer the essence of what it means to be a human being. Adolescents have a built-in search engine that is constantly seeking wholeness, if not signs of expansiveness and greatness, in the human beings that are part of their lives. When the search engine fails to locate these qualities, frustration and rage begins to brew. And, inevitably, the continuous search finds unworthy substitutes.

Many different factors have made the "absent parent syndrome" endemic in today's world. First, and perhaps foremost, the gradual crumbling of the communal structure in which all human beings once participated has put a tremendous burden on parents. At one time, nearly everyone lived within the context of a village, close to many members of their extended family. The burden of parenting was not the parents' alone. Grandparents, uncles, aunts, and often the entire community were part of the parenting effort.

While in Addis Ababa, Ethiopia in 1990, I remember encountering an Ethiopian Jew who had immigrated to Israel ten years previously. "What are you doing here?" I asked him. "I came to help my family immigrate to Israel," he told me. "How many people are in your family?" I asked. I knew that Ethiopians had large families and was well prepared for him to answer "eight" or "ten." "Eight hundred," was his answer. His concept of family reached back several generations, and, astonishingly, he knew every single member of his clan personally. Raising children within the bosom of such a tribe was a totally different experience than raising them within the constricted, well-defined boundaries of the nuclear family. The circle of the world, a world defined by a vast network of familial connections, affections and obligations, was something that existed naturally.

Can we recreate that circle for our teenagers and illuminate its contours within our shared world? Certainly, many parents, who themselves carry psychological wounds that may be expressed in a feeling of emptiness or alienation, may feel incapable of such a task. Yet, in my experience, the power to parent is something that is almost miraculously self-generating. It is as if this power is called into existence when an adult takes on the parental mantle and decides to manifest parental presence.

TULIA: THE SELF GENERATING MAGIC OF PARENTHOOD

Recently, I was reminded once again of the capacity of this mysterious magic called parenthood to appear out of nowhere. Among the latest group of orphans from Eastern European orphanages that Yemin Orde has taken in is an eight year old named Anatoly, or Tulia for short. Tulia's parents died in a car accident in Belarus when he was still an infant, and he was placed in a state-run orphanage. When he arrived at Yemin Orde in 2005, the Russian-speaking social worker who perused his documents recognized his family name; it was a rare one. She had helped care for an older man and his still more ancient mother—immigrants to Israel from Belarus—who shared the same name. Could there be a connection?

When we located the man, in his mid-sixties, and his 87-year-old mother, we found that they were, indeed, Tulia's grandfather and great grandmother. They had come to Israel in order to benefit from the pension and health-care services provided by the Israeli government to new immigrants. They had been certain that

Tulia was still in a state orphanage in Belarus and had no idea that he had made it to Israel and was living not far from them.

The social worker had remembered them as shut-ins who rarely left the closed circle of mother and son. They were sad, passive, and frightened people. The tiny apartment they inhabited, in a hard-scrabble neighborhood in Haifa, was dank and dark. At first they greeted the news that Tulia was in Israel with joy—but quickly, they became frightened that they would be given responsibility for raising him, something they felt financially and emotionally incapable of doing. Instead, we suggested that Tulia would come to visit them on weekends, but would remain in Yemin Orde during the week.

For Tulia's grandfather and great-grandmother, their new role in a child's life sparked a metamorphosis. Painstakingly, they cleaned out a small room for Tulia to sleep in when he came. They bought a lamp, decorated the walls with colored posters, and arranged for a desk and a computer for the boy. The other rooms of their apartment also began to brighten. So did their faces. They began to look forward to Tulia's visits all week, and they started to wish that he could spend more and more time with them. Tulia's unexpected re-entry into a family circle sped his process of social integration—from the moment he began to spend weekends with his family, his connection to the Israeli children in our village improved, as did his language skills and learning.

It was the older generation's transformation, however, that impressed me even more deeply. Before Tulia had come into their lives, his grandfather and great-grandmother had been feeble and forlorn, despondent, and incapable of running even their own lives. Tulia's presence had raised them to a new level of functioning, and bestowed upon them new emotional and spiritual energies. The light of parenthood, I saw once again, is capable of penetrating into very dark places.

THE STREAM OF LIFE PASSES BETWEEN GENERATIONS

The modern era has created conditions of separation and absence even within the circumscribed contemporary family unit—what we call the nuclear family. In the traditional village, children could see their parents plowing the fields, tending the livestock, or drawing water from the well, and often participated in these activities from an early age. In contrast, the modern work world is a place mostly cordoned off from the presence of children. At the turn of the 20th century the renowned thinker and educator John Dewey warned that the rift that had opened up between the world of work and that of family threatened to desiccate the educational endeavor by cutting it off from the natural flow of community and life. This trend has intensified. During the first two thirds of the 20th century it was usually only the father who spent long hours at work, and often he came home physically exhausted or preoccupied with paperwork and office politics. Now it has become common for both mother and father to work full time soon after a child's birth, and for both to be involved in demanding careers. The specialization that is a feature of modern jobs means that children often don't even fully understand what their parents do in the many hours they spend away from home.

The demands of work and career, and the mental and physical exhaustion that so often accompanies these demands, may cause children to view their parents as one-dimensional, and thus, in a deeper sense, absent. Most of us sacrifice a great deal of our time, our resources and our freedom, in order to raise and support our children—be they our biological children or those who have been put under our care as educators. Sometimes this knowledge, along with our inability to imagine an alternative way of raising these children, can cause us to deny the extent to which our involvement in their lives is governed by our efforts to be practical and efficient or to find our own forms of fulfillment. We may tell ourselves that our ultimate fulfillment lies in our children's present and future well-being, but too often we do not act accordingly. Much of our psychic energy is wrapped up in organizing ourselves around the need to function in an increasingly complicated world.

Yet if we are too fully immersed in the demands of an increasingly alienated social and economic world—the world that needs mending—it will rob us of our ability to radiate a fuller presence that can be absorbed into our children's hearts. As educators and as parents, we can and must develop the ability to separate ourselves, even for a moment at a time, from the stream of life and to relate to ourselves as entities that have that gift of "parenthood"—again, whether biological or not—built into our system. We may indeed feel overwhelmed; we may even experience our own life as shattered. Even so, it is possible, and necessary, to separate our own self-perception—which may be characterized by confusion, despair, or incoherence—from our sense of ourselves as parents. We may think that if we feel a sense of brokenness, this is the only thing we can transmit to our children. That is simply not true. The wholeness of parenthood is in our DNA.

Unless we insist on staking out a different kind of territory in our consciousness, by re-adopting a village state of mind as a basic orientation, day-to-day pressures and temptations will tend to triumph over all else in placing their stamp upon our lives, despite our elaborate strategies of denial. The children in our care intuitively understand when our primary concern is with ongoing life challenges not relating to them on the one hand—our social lives, for instance—and the technical "management" of their lives on the other hand. Such adults often are perceived by teenage children as external forces intent on imposing their own will and who are always ready to retreat from the distraction children pose to the fulfillment of their adult obligations or desires. In many cases, even those of us who really do feel that these children are of the utmost importance are forced to surrender to the exigencies of modern life.

DMITRI: *THIN WALLS AND CONSEQUENCES*

The story that follows may seem far-fetched. But it is an example of the way in which good parents can be totally unaware of how what they do for their own survival impacts their children. It is intended to be a bold reminder, for those of us who need it, of how necessary it is for adults to consider the impact of their choices on their children.

One particularly handsome young resident of Yemin Orde was named Dmitri, the only son of a divorced woman who had immigrated with him from the former Soviet Union. Dmitri, however, was reluctant to spend any of his weekends at home with her. After several discussions, he finally told me why. Dmitri's mother, an attractive, well-coifed woman, always had a man in her life, despite her difficulty in forming a long-term relationship. Being with a man, even in a temporary way, gave her a sense of security and well-being. But her son was not part of the exchange—love for security—that she offered her boyfriends.

Dmitri's mother truly loved her son. She wanted to be a good mother, and so she insisted that he return from our village periodically on weekends. She cared about his studies, his health, and his emotional life. She bought him clothes and cooked him his favorite foods. But the walls of her apartment were paper-thin, and she did not clearly think through the consequences of entertaining her boyfriends while Dmitri was at home. The result was that, while he was trying to sleep, he would often hear the moans of his mother and whoever her current lover was, and these sounds haunted him. It was as if his mother had two voices that he found difficult to separate, and even more problematic to reconcile: the calm, caring voice of the loving mother and the dark, throaty noises of passionate embrace. The intermingling of these voices confused and disturbed Dmitri. And, in fact, his mother's behavior attested to her unconscious refusal to take full responsibility for her place in Dmitri's life. Her desire to keep a man in her life would intermittently eclipse everything else, making Dmitri and his feelings as invisible as the dark side of the moon.

Could even the greatest dramatist express the inner plight of young Dmitri, whose hormones were swirling and boiling with increasing intensity, as images of sexual passion are superimposed over the likeness of his loving mother? Dmitri's own survival choice was to attempt to separate from his mother completely—thus his refusal to spend weekends at home. Even under conditions of greater stability and privacy than were available to Dmitri and his mother, modern parents often are not fully aware of the way their moods and behavior affect their children.

HAVE PARENTS LOST THEIR CONFIDENCE?

We tend to think, or perhaps it is convenient for us to think, that we influence our children only or chiefly through our direct interaction with them. Yet there is a limit to the extent to which we can compartmentalize the lives we share with our teenagers, as the story of Dmitri and his mother show. The temptation to cordon off our lives into distinct and separate units and functions can prevent real emotional contact from happening even within the family unit. Diversions pull our attention away from each other. We all know that our homes are no longer womb-like sanctuaries, but have been penetrated by electronic connections to the outside world that funnel attention away from children. The time and space in which family members can encounter each other is diminished, replaced by activities like watching television, talking on the telephone or surfing the Internet, in which individuals are transported into realms of virtual experience that are transpiring mostly in their own minds. The American cultural critic Neil Postman, in

The End of Education and other works, has drawn much public attention through his alarming, even devastating portrayal of the way in which contemporary forms of media have paralyzed and blocked our relationships with our children and our ability to educate.

These characteristic changes in the way people live increase the likelihood that parents will be perceived by their children as absent—as failing to provide the specific quality, the magical elixir of parenthood that teenagers crave. These quasi-technical explanations dovetail with an even more profound contemporary trend. The syndrome of the parent who is absent even while present can be traced to a widespread loss of confidence on the part of parents in their very ability to be parents. To understand this phenomenon at its roots, let us return to the example of the village—after all, it is in villages or other small communal units that the vast majority of human beings lived for thousands of years.

Within the village, the parent's role beyond insuring their progeny's immediate survival was clear: to transmit to the younger generation the wisdom of the past and prepare them to be self-confident members of the community and heads of their own family units. A significant part of today's parents' helplessness stems from the challenge of fulfilling this task, for which mankind, after countless generations of history, has been innately programmed. Like an incoming tide on a shore full of sandcastles, the modern period, beginning with the industrial and scientific revolutions, has swept away longstanding attitudes towards past and future that created the context for the relationship between generations. Our lives are, for the most part, not shaped by tradition anymore. The skills we need in order to survive are not, at least superficially, the same skills that our parents and grandparents used. Neither are the accepted values that shape our social lives. As the pace of technological and economic changes accelerates, our view of the past and of the future is blurred like the landscape seen from the window of a high-speed train.

MIRIAM: *THE COLLATERAL DAMAGE OF HISTORY*

The fast moving events that characterize our period can un-ravel the social fabric from which families draw their strength, thrusting children into paralyzing uncertainty. Take the story of Miriam, a young woman from an illustrious Jewish family that had been living in Persia, which now is Iran, for many genera-tions. Miriam's grandfather was a tailor for the Shah of Iran, in charge of a large staff whose mission was to provide the royal court with suitably lavish yet dignified garb. Miriam's grandfa-ther became wealthy enough to invest in real estate, eventually owning seven houses in and around Teheran. Miriam's father was a neurologist with a busy and lucrative practice. Her uncles and aunts on both sides were engineers, merchants and lawyers.

Then two things happened, almost simultaneously. In 1979 the Shah fell, and with him, the family's connections with the top level of the Iranian hierarchy was lost. The position "Tailor to the Royal Court," and the entire world of pomp and privilege it symbolized, disappeared. Most of Miriam's extended family left Iran for America, Italy, or Israel.

During this same period Miriam's father was in a car ac-cident, an accident for which the Iranian courts blamed him. Three women were killed in the accident, and Miriam's father had to pay a huge settlement to their families. All seven houses had to be sold in order to pay for the damage caused by a mo-ment of bad luck.

Miriam's father turned inward, closed his medical offices, and agreed to see only a few patients from his home. He grew silent and passive. In the newly tense and mournful household, only quarreling interrupted the silence. Miriam's mother and father, who had once lived harmoniously, had begun to fight. All this impacted Miriam in an immediate and palpable way.

She began to fail at her schoolwork, and was unable to make friends in the new school that she began to attend. She felt that her family, which once had seemed open and vibrant, attached to the outside world through a multiplicity of links, had become a sealed room—and that her mouth had been sealed along with it. Since she was a small child, she had hoped to follow in the footsteps of her uncles and aunts, and train as an engineer or medical doctor, but now she began to give up hope in the future. Finally, she decided that her only hope was to leave Iran and her gloomy household, following a beloved uncle to Israel.

Here circles of acquaintance and connection began to turn again in favor of Miriam. A Ministry of Education official who Miriam encountered while in search of a high school to attend was himself from Teheran and knew Miriam's family. Stunned to learn that the family fortune was now depleted, he sent her to Yemin Orde, where I promised her mother, who had accompanied her to Israel, that I would take care of her and give her everything she needed. Slowly she emerged from the shell in which her father's silence had enclosed her. Within the security of our village she was able to focus her efforts on learning to communicate, creating relationships with other young people. Eventually, she regained her lost confidence, and was able to free herself from her father's tragedy and reconnect to earlier, happier familial accomplishments from which she drew hope and ambition.

CENTER OF GRAVITY WITHIN THE GLOBAL VILLAGE

In many ways, the teenage struggle for identity is a struggle to find a past that has become passive and silent like Miriam's father after the accident. Human beings living in traditional societies often thought of their ancestors as giants. The legendary events of their tribes' collective pasts resonated with significance and meaning for their own lives. In popular conception today it is the present, with all its attention-grabbing, sense-arousing stimuli, and its revolutions in technology and style, that is representative of a fully vibrant life—everything that happened in the past is seen as faded and slightly irrelevant.

The representation of the world as a place whose elements are constantly being improved and made over is at the root of the powerful marriage between technological advance and the consumer society. Western-style consumerism, in which products are constantly reinvented and re-presented as "new and improved," has an effect on parental self-confidence that is potent and widespread. Consumer culture and all that accompanies it has usurped, in important ways, the role that the village and its traditions and elders once filled—the presentation, interpretation and mediation of the world to the younger generation. There is a reason that the spread of Western mass culture to nearly every corner of the world is a phenomenon that is popularly known as the creation of "a global village." Films, television, news shows, magazines, the Internet, and fashion are part of a single oscillating surface, a colossal distorting mirror that purports to show young people all over the globe what is important. Mass culture has taken over the function of the traditional village in interpreting and mediating the world and shaping the consciousness of our youngsters.

This might be a good thing, except that the forces that create this mass culture are not guided by the goal of forging and educating human souls. Instead, the form and content of mass culture are tools of the market, a way to sell products through the hypnotic sheen of style and celebrity. The result is that our tools of communication are to a great extent devoted to sending us on a quest for instant gratification. There is little opportunity to escape from the images projected directly into our homes through the television, radio and Internet and into our communities through pervasive advertising. In the face of this tidal wave, parents can be forgiven for making the fatal mistake of believing that they have no chance to provide their children with an alternate or complementary structure of meaning.

One of the characteristics of mass media is that it offers itself to us blindly and without discrimination. This makes it nearly impossible for parents to protect children from what is inappropriate for them to see or know at particular stages of development. We can try hard to limit the hours they watch television, or put filtering programs on our Internet servers, but like the walls in Dmitri's mother's apartment, the protective screens we put up for our children are too thin, and the din of mass culture too shrill. No matter how vigilantly we stand guard, its message will still, eventually, seep into our children's world.

This is what makes it imperative that we learn to create a space marked by clear contours in which the overwhelming influence of mass culture is neutralized and de-fanged. We do this by drawing within our minds the circle that represents the possibility of changing the world for the better, *Tikkun Olam*, thus reactivating from within the recesses of our memory the world of connectivity and caring that is part of the human legacy. As we become aware of the circle of *Tikkun Olam* we open up the space for a further, deeper, more personal dimension: the circle of *Tikkun HaLev*.

Where am I within these two circles, where is my center of gravity? How can I connect to myself? The horizontal and vertical lines help me answer these questions. I am a person rooted in my past, moving toward my future; this is the horizontal line. I am a person standing on the solid ground of the present, but my aspirations reach beyond my given reality; the vector of this line is vertical. The place where these lines meet provides the coordinates of my center of gravity. Using her built in GPS, which seeks meaning and direction, my adolescent is searching for this center of gravity within me—it is a place she can connect to, and recharge from, as if from a source of power. The circles and the lines thus position us in a center while marking off an area in which we have regained meaningful influence.

BEYOND AUTHORITY AND DISCIPLINE

It is important that we separate within our thinking the concepts of parental presence and influence from the notion of parental authority and discipline. The reassertion of parental influence will not succeed if it takes the shape of mere discipline that is experienced by teenagers as a form of arbitrary authority. Some recent "innovators" suggest a return to the strict hierarchy that once characterized relations between children and their parents and teachers. This kind of thinking should make us uneasy. Is returning to a relationship based on dominance really an option today? Does such a return represent progress, or is it merely a form of retreat and regression? Isn't it possible to take what we have learned about human relationships and our inner worlds and produce something better?

In fact, the depredations of arbitrary authority represent another characteristic sickness of the 20th century. Franz Kafka is, by some accounts, the greatest of modern literary geniuses because of his precise and haunting depiction of modern society. The heroes of his stories inhabit an alienated universe, whose atmosphere is one of vague but ominous threat. Kafka brilliantly depicts the impact on the human soul of a society that has developed a strict bureaucratic structure of control but has lost its sense of meaning. Joseph K., the central figure of Kafka's masterpiece, *The Trial*, is never able to determine the nature of the crime for which he is being judged, and yet still is filled with feelings of guilt and shame up until his very last moment, when he is executed "like a dog."

Kafka's description of the horrific possibilities of modern life was based on his keen intuitions about social and political trends, which seem almost prophetic in light of the universes of totalitarian terror that Hitler and Stalin began to unleash within a decade or so of his death. But there was also a personal and psychological dimension to the desperation of Kafka's characters. The key to this dimension can be found in Kafka's autobiographical *Letter to My Father*, in which a young man tells of his father's tyrannical influence. The father depicted in the book is so obnoxiously domineering that no room remains within the son's psyche in which his own, independent view of reality can develop. Only the humiliating power of the Father's authority holds the world together. In the absence of Father, the world would crumble into a million separate pieces.

CHAOS IS NOT OUR DESTINY

What is the relationship between the alienated world of *The Trial* and the corrosive model of parenting described in *Letter to My Father*? One of the deep truths that emerge from Kafka's work is that the social and psychological worlds—the realms of *Tikkun Olam* and *Tikkun HaLev*—constantly interpenetrate. Parent-child and educator-child relations based on domination and fear have a toxic impact on a social atmosphere already supercharged with estrangement and threat. But if we succeed in creating a world together with our children in which our role as guide or mediator is not arbitrary, but emanates from shared structures of meaning and from a sense of togetherness, we have a chance to roll back the spread of Kafka's alienated world. Our children will not have the nebulous sense of guilt that makes Joseph K. passive in the face of injustice. They will have an affinity with those aspects of contemporary reality that symbolize the promise of hope.

THE VILLAGE STATE OF MIND

In this regard, we should take the African proverb, "It takes a village to raise a child" to heart. Yet what a child needs is not the village itself, but the dimensions and values that are embedded in the life of the village—what we have called "the village state of mind." Adolescents' consciousness of time is often simply a reaction to stimuli from the present. But a consciousness of time limited to the present is at the heart of many negative behaviors that teenagers can exhibit—especially addiction and violence. Adolescents, then, must see themselves as part of something larger than themselves, as significant links in the chain of universal human existence.

The past has a strong presence in the village in the form of the elderly and their life stories, in the historical memory carried by the members of the village, in stories about ancestors, and in all the traditional cultural practices. We have to ensure that our child's existential present is anchored in the past, just as the village is. Indeed, while we have to allow space for our kids to be angry at having been deprived of growing up with their own families, our own efforts must focus on addressing the past in a way that will help them draw strength from it. The future is present in the village in the sense that the village is a self-perpetuating way of life. Children and adolescents see, in the fabric of daily life, how older children learn skills, are given responsibility, and are initiated into the mysteries of adult life, and they know that their turn will come. Our children, too, must feel that they have a stake in the future.

In the face of the tides of the contemporary world, which can sweep from our lives all evidence of the past and annihilate our sense of time as a continuum, we can restore the presence of the past in our children's lives. We can ease the threat our children experience because of the uncertain nature of the personal and communal future in our world by reassuring them that we will be there for them when they need us. We can provide them with a platform that frees them from anxiety and fear and facilitates the dynamic exploration of the world in which they are fated to live. We create around us an illuminated circle into which we can grow and expand, thus encircling our children. The story of Enrique illustrates how that circle can be created, if it is absent, or how it can be repaired if it needs mending.

ENRIQUE: *YEMIN ORDE ABOVE AND BELOW*

Enrique was a teen who came to Yemin Orde Youth Village from destitution in Brazil. His mother, a young woman from an Orthodox Jewish family, had been disowned by her parents after running away with a young mulatto man she had met at "Carnival." When he abandoned her while she was pregnant with Enrique, she was forced to support herself and her infant child by cleaning the offices of a large travel agency in Rio de Janeiro. When Enrique was four years old, his mother placed him in the Lar da Crianca Jewish orphanage. From there he eventually reached our Village in Israel. As part of our efforts to heal and mend Enrique's relationship with his mother, we brought her to Israel for the summer. For the first time since he was an infant, Enrique was able to spend time with his mother in a safe environment. They were able to explore their relationship and iron out the hurt he had felt when she abandoned him. During her stay, Enrique was able to condense his life and his mother's into one intense summer, as if reliving all that he had missed as a child. It was a summer of turbulent fights and emotional reconciliation. Every day new wounds opened and old wounds healed. In the village, he had found a place where his basic needs were taken care of, and that implanted in him some sense of security about his future, which enabled him to absorb his mother's narrative with compassion.

When Enrique left Yemin Orde and continued on his life's

journey he chose to give me a present: a sculpture in the form of a stone-carved open book titled "The Book of My Life." The letters of most of the first page were black and blurry. Little by little, the letters gained clarity and color, until finally they were bright and multicolored like a rainbow.

"The colored letters represent my life story from the time I came to Yemin Orde," he told me. Enrique later said, in his usual lyrical way, that for him there are two Yemin Ordes. There is the actual Yemin Orde that as a graduate he sometimes visits; and there is the ideal Yemin Orde, which he carries around in his heart. He was alluding to a notion he had encountered in a course on Jewish mystical thought. According to tradition, there are two Jerusalems—one below and one above, the earthly Jerusalem and the heavenly Jerusalem. While the earthly Jerusalem has rocks, roads, buildings and dust, the heavenly one is more of a perfect ideal than an actual place. Still, the two Jerusalems are reflected in each other.

Enrique and many of those lucky enough to have had an adolescence that gave them the opportunity to recover from traumatic childhood experiences carry with them the years of healing and transformation as a representation of a perfect ideal; their heavenly Jerusalem. This new and ancient ideal of the human community as an embracing vortex and crucible is what we have called "the Village state of mind."

Finding our parental center of gravity means first regaining confidence in our role as mentors. We have to counter the teenager's perception that her parents have lost faith in their own ability to be parents. Once we have overcome the initial shock of parenthood, our small children evoke in most of us an instinctual confidence. We know what to do with them. When they cry, we can lift them easily in our arms and hug them until their crying stops. To entertain and teach our little ones, we can carry them on our backs to the zoo, watch them as they play on the seesaw, fascinate them with simple fairy tales, sing them lullabies, and teach them to read.

With our teenage children, we often feel as if we do not know what to do with them anymore. They're too big. They want too many contradictory things. The volume and intensity of their emotions may be frightening. We lose confidence—and they feel it. They lash out against us, testing us, as if thrashing about in quicksand hoping to feel a solid bottom.

Of course even with infants modern society "succeeded," at least for a time, in weakening our natural parental instincts in a most dramatic way. For several long decades, some 20th century "experts" on scientific child rearing convinced millions of mothers that breast-feeding was an archaic practice that was at best primitive and unnecessary and at worst could do permanent psychological harm. Nursing came to be considered, in some circles, something almost obscene, and was banned from the public sphere as if it were a deviant act. Now, of course, we know that mothers pass on to their children much more than just milk when they nurse—both physically, by providing essential components of a healthy immune system, and emotionally. Because we since have been convinced of the importance of nursing for a baby's physical and psychological development, parents have insisted on restoring its legitimate place in child rearing.

We need to do the same thing with the parental presence in teenage lives. We need to restore self-confidence in our own instincts, our inner knowledge that our multi-dimensional presence is of unique importance in our teenage children's development. We need to internalize the knowledge that our job as parents is not finished until our children are functioning adults, and we must renew our belief in our ability to carry the task of parenting through until its goal has been reached.

OVERCOMING SEPARATION ANXIETY

When our teenagers sense our lack of self-confidence as parents, it heightens their anxiety that we will continue to withdraw emotionally from them. One of the notable insights that the cross-fertilization of psychology and biology has contributed to 20th century thought is the notion of separation anxiety as a guiding emotional principle of the human psyche. According to John Bowlby, the American psychoanalytic theorist who was influenced by both the disciplines of psychology and animal development, the fear of abandonment is one of the basic components of the psyche of any animal raised by parents. Bowlby's insight was remarkable in its simplicity. Animals desperately need their parents, both for nourishment and protection, and to learn the basics of survival, of how to be the particular kind of animal they are meant to become. Birds, mammals, and certainly humans, do not learn in a vacuum, but through a close and intensive relationship with a parent. Nearly from the moment of birth, animal and human infants are in a state of distress when separated from their mothers, and they wait anxiously for what Bowlby calls "The safe return of the mother."

This most basic emotion is not something that disappears completely as animals and human beings grow up. The imprint of separation anxiety is so deep that it continues to be a potent force in children, teenagers, and even in the adult psyche. Healing separation anxiety is one of the core challenges of *Tikkun HaLev*, or fixing the inner circle of the heart. Separation anxiety morphs into many forms and appears as a factor in nearly every kind of relationship. In the relationship between parent and teenager, the separation anxiety of each side feeds on that of the other side. Teenagers fear parental abandonment. At least part of the meaning of provocative teenage behavior is that the teenager is testing the parent in order to affirm or negate their worst fears; namely, that their parent will reject and abandon them.

Parents, for their part, also often fear abandonment. They fear that their children will reject them, or already are in the process of rejecting them. This fear connects with the fear of abandonment they carry with them from infancy, a fear that is a ubiquitous part of human development, but that has been complicated by the myriad negative experiences most people endure as they grow up. Part of becoming the kind of parental presence our children need in their lives means overcoming our fear of rejection and separation. The fear of rejection and separation is part of what keeps us emotionally withdrawn from our teenagers, just as it keeps them provoking and testing our commitment to them.

Acting In versus Acting Out

To a great extent, then, adolescent "acting out" is a response to the lopsided equation between abandonment and maternal return in the world they are growing into. There is far too much abandonment—divorce, anomie, unpredictable change, parental absence, breakdown of community—and far too little embrace and reassurance, which are the elements of reality that could represent for the teenagers the safe return of the mother. The sense of a reality flooded by abandonment maddens teenagers, makes them strike out blindly at the generation that brought them into the world but has retreated from their responsibility of providing guidance in how to live.

In the face of teenage acting out, parents have to learn to "act in." Expanding our presence in our teenagers' lives does not mean reacting to provocation with threats and punishments. Instead, we have to turn inward, at least initially, becoming aware of our own power, and the possibility we have to counter absence with meaningful presence, emptiness with content, and abandonment with embrace. In order for any of this to happen, we have to allow ourselves to be touched inside by the challenge of parenthood. We have to understand that the parent-child relationship is not a one-way street. On a deep level, our teenagers offer us a chance to mine our own souls, our own history and our own convictions in order to bring ourselves fully into the parent-child relationship.

Not least, through our teenagers we receive the opportunity to reach back into our own teenage years. This is not a book about parenting, per se. Still, we have found through long experience that children with no parents or absent parents require reliable representations of parental wholeness to thrive. Indeed, parental qualities in educators are inseparable from quality education. Learning to become aware of the circle of *Tikkun HaLev* in the context of parenting, we attend to our own shattered hearts. If our teenage years were troubled, we have the chance to heal ourselves. We can do this by focusing our inner awareness and achieving sufficient understanding so that we do not reproduce our own negative experiences, passing them on to our children. If our teenage years were good ones, we cannot simply take it for granted that our children will have the same experience. We have to tap into that goodness, and transmit it to our children.

GARDEN OF THE LATE BLOOMERS

The inward journey we need to take as educators performing some of the roles of parenthood is not psychological but relational. It will not focus on the isolated individual psyche, but on how our inner experiences and emotional depths touch those of these children, and vice versa. That is why I believe it is important to share what I have learned about the significance of parents in the eyes of their children from years of experience directing a youth village for children from disadvantaged or immigrant populations. Many of the teenagers in our village come from families plagued by divorce, abandonment, or violence. Quite a few are children from the former Soviet Union who, because of their circumstances, have chosen to live in Israel without their parents. Others are the children of Ethiopian immigrants whose parents never fully adjusted to life in Israel, are chronically unemployed, illiterate, and speak only a broken Hebrew.

One might assume that as director of the Yemin Orde Youth Village, where I am often forced to take on a quasi-parental role, I would have developed a perspective in which the importance of biological parenthood is diminished. Some educators, including some I admire, have adopted such a view. A.S. Neill expresses disdain for parents in his classic book *Summerhill*. Neill's ambition at the Summerhill

School was to create a school community where children could be safely detoxified from what he considered the often poisonous influence of their parents. I think that Neill was right about some important things, among them his belief in the primacy of children's emotional lives over intellectual achievement as a goal of education and his emphasis on liberating children from fear. But on the issue of parents he was dead wrong. We are used to talking about paternal and maternal instincts, but there is an instinct at least as deeply rooted within children's hearts that holds their relationship to their parents as important almost regardless of who the parents are. As an educator in a youth village, my position has given me a unique vantage point from which to perceive the hunger children have for their parents. If there is one thing I have learned during my years as an educator, it is how profoundly parents figure in their children's mind and hearts.

It is important for parents and teachers to realize that *children never really give up on parental figures.* This may come as big news to some of us, because teenagers are notoriously hard on their parents. During the years of adolescence, rebellion and independence are part of the teenager's basic developmental agenda. Teenagers test themselves and their newfound power against their parents, and often challenge their parents' authority and beliefs. What is less well known is that while all this is going on, somewhere in the depth of the child's psyche, the connection to her parents, the purity of her love and admiration for her parents, and the deep desire to make her parents proud never fades. This insight must be carved into the hearts of everyone involved in raising or educating teenagers.

We can illustrate this through the story of three roommates, two Eastern European immigrants and one native Israeli, who between them had parents who represented the most severe kinds of absence and dysfunction, and yet who refused to write them off.

IVAN: RECONSTRUCTING FATHER

First, there was Ivan. His father, while married to another woman, had impregnated Ivan's mother in Russia, and had moved to Israel shortly afterwards. Fifteen years later, Ivan came to Israel and enrolled at Yemin Orde, never having met or heard from his father. Over the next year, Ivan searched for his father, only to be told by the Ministry of the Interior that his father was dead and buried in a cemetery in central Israel. Ivan went to the cemetery and, after searching for hours, found his father's grave. On the grave he placed a note, inside a clear plastic cover to protect it from rain, saying that he was this man's son and that he would welcome contact with anyone who knew him.

Six months later, he got a phone call. It was his half-sister, already married and with children of her own. Neither Ivan nor his sister had known about each other's existence until she had found the note on their father's grave. Ivan and his sister became very close friends, and spent hours talking about the father they shared, whom the sister had known well. Together, they "reconstructed" the father, giving him new life through their discussions. Ivan's search for his father, and the portrait of his father that he eventually was able to piece together, was an important step for him in solidifying his own sense of identity.

YAAKOV: NOT EVEN TOTAL REJECTION

Ivan had a roommate, Yaakov, who was a strikingly beautiful young man who had also spent his childhood in Russia. Yaakov's father and mother had divorced when Yaakov was eight, and his father, on the verge of immigrating, offered to take Yaakov to Israel with him. Like many eight-year olds, Yaakov was attached to his mother and decided to stay with her. His father treated this as a grievous insult. Yaakov's mother eventually died, and

Yaakov moved to Israel and Yemin Orde, but his father refused to see him. Yaakov would travel to the town where his father lived—a two-hour journey—and knock on the door. His father would open the door, see his handsome son, and slam the door on him. Remarkably, Yaakov refused to say a bad word about his father during all of our discussions with him. As much as I found his father's behavior abhorrent, I was amazed by Yaakov's loyalty. Not even total rejection could extinguish the flame of love he held for his father.

ELI: YOU DIDN'T MISS THE TRAIN

Ivan and Yaakov's third roommate was an Israeli named Eli, whose mother had been committed to a mental hospital after numerous psychotic episodes. Eli's story is the most complicated, both because he was the most troubled of the three roommates and because his love for his mother was submerged below the surface of his personality for a number of years. As a child, Eli had been passed around from the home of one of his mother's relatives to another, until finally he landed in our village. Periodically, Eli's mother would escape the hospital ward and arrive unannounced on the grounds of Yemin Orde, in search of her son—eager to make sure that he was doing alright, and wanting to talk to me and to his teachers to ensure that he was progressing in his studies. Her clothes were disheveled and saliva often dribbled down from the side of her mouth onto her chin. Eli would run away every time his mother showed up. After she left, he would almost invariably engage in some kind of destructive misbehavior. He liked to set fires, to steal, and to talk back to teachers.

Soon after Eli came to our village, I told him my "secret" in a conscious effort to form a bond between the two of us. My mother, too, had been insane. This knowledge formed the basis of a covenant of trust between us. Subtly, through the tone of voice with which I spoke about my mother, I tried to convey to him that loving an insane mother was a legitimate, even a healthy, choice.

Eli could always reach me when he needed to talk, and even though his behavior often bordered on madness, I saw that there was a basic element of goodness and normalcy in his personality. His friends trusted him—and in some strange way, I trusted him as well. Sometimes, when he seemed to be particularly agitated, his counselors feared that he might do himself or others harm. He seemed to sense their worry and he would seek me out. "You don't have to lose any sleep tonight over me," he would say. And I believed him.

At Yemin Orde, each of the twenty residential houses where the children sleep and live is named after a great figure from Jewish or general history. Eli lived in the Abraham Lincoln house. One day his counselor called me and told me to come to the house quickly. When I got there, I saw what Eli had done. In huge letters alongside the name "Abraham Lincoln House," he had added another name. The sign now also read, "Eli Mousayef House."

I was secretly pleased. To me, Eli's massive graffiti meant that he really did feel at home in the Village, and also that he had dreams of greatness. Along with discussions of the seriousness involved in damaging communal property, and our insistence on Eli repairing the damage he had done, I managed to slip in a line that showed him that I recognized and affirmed his dreams. "Someday there will be a Eli Mousayef house," I joked with him.

A year or so later came another incident that further tested our relationship. Eli was in the habit of attending school and synagogue services intermittently—only when he felt like it. I had given his counselors and teachers instructions to let him sleep in when he felt like it. One Saturday morning, our Sabbath, while nearly the entire population of the Village was in synagogue for Sabbath prayers, someone had tortured and beheaded a cat. Its burnt and headless carcass was found as we walked back from synagogue. All signs pointed to Eli as the perpetrator. His mother had made one of her dramatic appearances in the Village just the day before, and aside from her disturbing demeanor, the counselors knew that Eli came undone after nearly every one of his mother's visits. As soon as Eli understood what had happened, and that he was the prime suspect, he ran off into the woods surrounding our village and disappeared.

The staff believed that Eli's flight was another indication that it was he who had slain the cat, but something about the whole story didn't make sense to me. I had never seen that kind of cruelty in him and I didn't believe it existed. After the staff had searched for him for a whole day in the forest, I went out carrying a bullhorn. "I know you didn't do it," I announced. "I know you didn't do it." Nearly immediately, I found him. He had camouflaged himself in a pile of leaves, but had responded right away to my faith in him by emerging from his hiding place. As it turned out, Eli had not tortured and killed the cat. This terrible act had been carried out by a visitor, the brother of one of our resident youths, who had run away from a drug rehabilitation program and come to Yemin Orde for refuge.

The next year, his senior year, Eli began to emerge from his cocoon. Like someone waking up to bright sunlight and realizing that he had missed the early train to work, Eli saw his friends taking the matriculation exams that would qualify them for college or university, and realized, as if for the first time, that actions carry with them long-term consequences. He came to me in a state of despair. "I've missed my chance," he said, "It's too late."

What would have happened to him if I had conveyed to him that he had, indeed, already missed the train? That his life could no longer be a success story? I sometimes refer to our village as a garden of the late bloomers because so many of our teenagers—like teenagers the world over—are wrapped in cocoons, dealing with traumatic childhood experiences and healing from them during the early years of adolescence. Only later are they capable of devoting themselves to building their futures. The trick is to be there for these teenagers when they are ready to bloom.

"This year is an important year," I told Eli. "If you work hard this year, we'll help you catch up."

Eli did work hard, and became a member of our first class at the Mechina, a gap-year program that was designed for our late bloomers, enabling them to make up study materials they had missed and prepare for the mandatory three years in the Israeli army. It was as if all the energy that seemed to have been wasted during Eli's teenage years had actually been stored up inside him, and it burst outwards now in great abundance. Eli succeeded in his studies, and at the same time took on enormous responsibility—organizing the buying and cooking of food for the entire 45-person program.

At the end of the year, the Mechina youth take a long and arduous hike, at the end of which they arrive at their graduation ceremony. Eli's mother was there to greet him as he finished the hike, carrying the giant flag, exhausted but exhilarated from the effort of the walk, and from the effort he had made to transform his life. This time he did not turn away from his mother, though her appearance was as jarring as ever. I was near enough to hear their conversation, which was touching and heartbreaking at the same time.

"Here's 50 shekels," his mother said, shoving the money, the equivalent of about ten dollars, into Eli's hand. "Remember you owe me 50 shekels." And then she added something else, as if from a different layer of her persona. "You're the most precious thing in my life," she said softly.

He took the money. "Mom," he said. "I owe you a lot more than 50 shekels." His voice and eyes gave clear evidence of the love for his mother that he had hidden all these years, hidden until he was strong enough to face her. For me, Eli's words and expression were evidence of the powerful, perhaps genetic instinct that draws children to their parents, and keeps them from rejecting them despite almost any circumstance.

GUARDIANS OF SHATTERED DREAMS

Rural Ethiopia is a society in which parental authority over children is nearly absolute. Here in Israel, Ethiopian parents are disempowered. The skills they bring with them from Ethiopia are little appreciated here in Israel; they often must survive on government aid. Children thus see parents who were once respected for their resourcefulness, wisdom and mastery of their environment drift into passivity, collecting welfare checks and developing psychosomatic diseases, like Shalom's father's asthma. Yet, it is rare to find an Ethiopian youngster who does not retain a deep and basic respect for his parents and elders. Many times I have seen Ethiopians, even those who are members of street gangs and have police records, become transformed the moment they enter their parents' homes. Dreadlocks, earrings, and all, they will hold their right forearm with their left hand and bow slightly, extending their right hand to their parents in the Ethiopian gesture of respect.

I will never forget the sight of Naftali Fantahon bending his head to kiss his father's knees during his graduation ceremony from the Technion. Naftali is one of the first Ethiopians ever to graduate as an engineer from Israel's highly prestigious college of science and technology. Naftali's father came to the graduation dressed in his traditional white clothes, an elderly man who never learned to read or to write even in his own language. For Naftali, kissing his father's knees was a gesture that honored his father as his source of life and origin.

I remember another youngster who never knew his father. His

mother was so retarded that she didn't have full control over her swallow function; saliva dribbled down her chin. He himself was a beautiful and talented young man, who bloomed into promising young adulthood here at Yemin Orde. And yet his mother was always a central part of his dreams. "Some day I am going to get an academic prize, in university," he would often tell me, "and my mother is going to see what sprang from her."

FLIES ON THE WALL

Raising teenagers can, indeed, be exhausting and frustrating—and often can leave us feeling like failures. We naturally tend to think that the arguments, insolence, rebelliousness and day-to-day manipulations of our teenagers tell the whole story of what they think of us. In actuality, all of these conflicts, though important, are secondary phenomena compared to the place that teenagers reserve in the depths of their heart for their parents. If we could be like flies on the wall and hear our teenagers talking about us to their friends, often times we would be in for a pleasant surprise, because it is so different from the insolent assessments of us which they sometimes throw in our face. It is as if children instinctively know what our religious traditions teach: that parents are partners with God in the creation of the world—the unique world of each child.

The hidden reverence of children for their parents is almost a religious feeling. Jewish commentators have long noted that the first part of the Ten Commandments deals with religious devotion—the belief in one God, the prohibitions against idolatry and blasphemy, and the commandment to keep the Sabbath day holy. Perhaps for this reason, "Honor thy father and mother" is part of the first half of the Ten Commandments—which focus on the human being's relationship to God—rather than the second half, which is about man's relationship to his fellow man. This built-in place in children's hearts puts parents in a position of tremendous responsibility and provides an amazing opportunity.

As the stories I've recounted demonstrate, parents are virtually never failures in their children's eyes, and parents who recover their good will towards their children will always get a second chance. Children, except in extreme cases, are always waiting for their parents to come through. Because their unconscious need for parental figures is so profound, children are always willing to give their parents a chance to rehabilitate themselves. Children are willing to pay a high price, risking deep disappointment, if there is a chance to renew contact or trust with a parental figure.

SALMON SWIMMING UPSTREAM

The instinct drawing adolescents towards parents is so strong that when it is frustrated, children look for substitutes. My own healing in adolescence involved such a search. First, expressing a desire to draw closer to the Jewish religious tradition, I asked my grandparents, who had always been an island of sanity in my world, if I could live with them so as to attend school in the heavily religious area in which they lived. Some of the children in the new school I had chosen sensed the weakness of my family background and began to scapegoat me. But a child named Simcha Fenster befriended and protected me, and brought me home to his parents.

Whereas the Nazi persecution had indirectly caused my mother's mental breakdown, the Fenster family's experience during the Holocaust was, remarkably, a source of strength for them. The Fensters had escaped into the wilderness ahead of the Nazi occupation of their hometown of Bratislava. They had carried their young children around with them on their backs as they moved from hiding place to hiding place. Because they felt a sense of gratitude and triumph at having been able to stay together as a family, they miraculously emerged from the Holocaust as whole people. I could feel this in their household, which was homey, orderly and sweet smelling, suffused with values, but also with pride in the family and what it represented. Mrs. Fenster was noble, delicate, and very natural in her appearance and her manner, and she and Mr. Fenster took a special interest in me.

Simcha had decided to attend high school in Kfar Haroeh, a religious boarding school headed by a charismatic rabbi, Moshe Zvi Neriah. When I decided to attend as well, Mr. Fenster went with me, acting as a surrogate parent. I remember clearly, as if engraved on my heart, the sight of Mr. Fenster carrying my battered suitcase for me towards the boarding school. The suitcase, upholstered, with stripes, represented for me my wanderings in search of a home. It was as if, in Mr. Fenster's small gesture of carrying my suitcase, he had lifted up my past—all the painful memories I carried with me—and transformed them by sharing their weight, thus breaking the taut cords of my loneliness.

At Kfar Haroaeh I met other surrogate parents. One was Rabbi Menachem Ofen, who had organized religious services right in the midst of a Nazi death camp, fasting on the Day of Atonement even though he was nearly starving. He, too, carried my suitcase. I had become frustrated and angry with the school and with myself, and I walked to the road dragging my belongings with me, intending to leave Kfar Haroeh forever. Rabbi Ofen ran after me, and with sweetness and determination attempted to convince me not to leave. Finally, as I stood there not knowing what to do, he picked up my eternal suitcase and carried it carefully back to my room.

Another influential surrogate family during my high-school years at Kfar Haroeh was that of Zvi Weinberg, a history teacher with a passion for his subject, exacting and yet full of sharp humor. Together with his wife Sitta, he was raising nine children. Mr. Weinberg had the mentality of a mentor, of someone for whom every encounter in the classroom was an occasion for transmitting not just knowledge, but a way of thinking. The emotional boundaries between the classroom and his home were porous. I knew very early in my experience in Kfar Haroaeh that what I was really looking for was family, not institutional life. The Weinberg home was a living connection for me between the life of the classroom and that of the family; open and stimulating enough to make me feel like I had indeed found a home. In fact, seven years later I married their youngest daughter, Shuli, and we eventually had five children of our own!

It is rare, though, for teachers to replace parents in children's hearts. I recall my own search for parental figures as something akin to an instinctual drive, like salmon swimming upstream to the place they were born, or birds migrating to safe shores for the winter. The force of this drive is something that all parents would do well to remember. Teenagers' struggle against their parents often is so fierce that parents might come to believe that the teenagers actually want to see their parents defeated, humiliated, or dislodged from their place in their children's lives. But deep down, teenagers want their parents to survive their onslaught. The defeat of a parent is a Pyrrhic victory for a teenager. Teenagers want their parents to be strong, even as they demand the right to reveal their own strength by testing it against that of their parents. Shifting the way parents and educators see their teenagers will empower them enormously, and allow them to survive the teenage onslaught. This shift of vision involves seeing the total context of teenagers' lives, and developing a new perspective on their role as guides and touchstones for their children.

Where do children get this intense desire to share their triumphs with their parents, no matter who their parents are? To me it seems that children are the silent guardians of their parents' shattered dreams. They carry, as if in their genetic code, their parents' unfulfilled potential.

6

SECOND BIRTH:
ENCIRCLING IS EMBRACING

The life of a young Ethiopian boy living far from the city in a traditional society was quite different from the regimented and protected life of most teenagers in the West. From the age of 12, a boy like Tedesse, our young math student, might be given responsibility for a flock of sheep. For several weeks, he would wander with the sheep in a circular route through meadows and over hills, seeking fresh pastureland and sources of pure water, exploring the countryside, experiencing his independence, and testing his own physical skills and powers of judgment against the elements.

Yet at all times Tedesse would be connected to the traditions and expectations of his culture. His adventure would take place within the context of service to his family and his village. The wool, milk and meat that the sheep he kept alive provided were essential for the survival and wellbeing of his people, and as such, also would provide a place for him in life. Often, in village society, young men and women were married off to each other between the ages of 12 and 16. But rather than start a fully independent household, they would move in with either the bride or groom's family, beginning their lives as fledgling adults within the protected circle formed by their elders.

Our understanding of teenagers today would be enriched if we compare the context in which we now live to the traditional world that preceded it. The structure of our psyche has not radically changed. The emotional needs and expectations that have developed over thousands of years of human civilization were not suddenly erased by the abrupt and rapid spread of urban, industrial society. Emotionally, we still live in expectation of the structures of meaning and community that have accompanied the development of human life from time immemorial.

To a great extent, adolescence as we know it now is a phenomenon of the modern world. Whereas in traditional society sexual maturity, marked by various kinds of rites of passage, began an entirely new period in a person's life, the industrial revolution caused an extension of childhood for an additional period of 5 to 8 years beyond the onset of sexual maturity. At first, this lengthening of some aspects of childhood was confined to the upper classes. These classes understood that if their children were to retain their privileged place within the emerging social structure of the modern world, they would have to undergo a longer period of learning and honing of skills.

For a long time, adolescence and the concept of secondary school education that accompanied it were solely upper class phenomena. Teenagers from the lower classes worked from an early age—in factories, farms, or as apprentices to craftsmen of various kinds. Eventually, at least in the West, as democracy and the demand for equal opportunity spread, child labor was outlawed and secondary education began to be accepted as a norm in all sectors of society. To this day in developing countries child labor is common, and often, in lower-class families in Western society, adolescents—especially young women—bear a greater share of responsibility for the welfare of the household than do teenagers from more privileged homes.

Adolescence, then, has drastically changed in meaning over the last few centuries. In the West, at least, it has come to designate a period when physical and mental powers are highly developed, but familial and economic responsibilities remain, basically, those of children. This state of conflicting status—again, mainly for Western teenagers—is another major source of the obsessive search for identity that has come to characterize the teenage years in Western society.

Societal changes have in many ways created adolescence as we know it. Still, the period that followed the physical and sexual maturing of a child has always had a special status. In the Talmud, a compendium of laws and ethical and spiritual teachings that was set down by Jewish sages some 1,500 years ago, children are considered adults when they reach sexual maturity; for boys, on the average, at the age of 13 and for girls at the age of 12. According to Jewish law, a 13-year-old who damages property, murders, or commits some other offence can be held fully accountable in the courtroom. But, the Talmud adds, this is not the case under divine law. Human courts must prosecute teenage offenders, in order to maintain the social order. But God recognizes the moratorium of adolescence. Only from the age of 20 is a person liable for punishment from heaven for his misdeeds. In ancient society, teenagers married, worked and took on responsibility, and thus had to be held liable for their actions. But from the perspective of heaven, teenagers were still children in the process of forging their soul.

In the kabbalistic corpus of the 16th century Safed School of Jewish mysticism, the beginning of the teenage years are likened to the embryonic period before birth—they are literally termed "a second period of pregnancy." Adult consciousness is present in the early teenage years as a kind of seed that must be nurtured and developed. Only when parents feel confident enough in their offspring's grasp of reality to allow them to serve as agents in managing the family's financial resources (usually around the age of 20) is full adult consciousness considered to have been reached. As we shall see, this Kabbalistic idea is strikingly similar to those of some modern psychological and educational thinkers.

Teenagers are Outcasts

Before the development of modern adolescence, the early teen-age years were a time for self-discovery. This is still the case in the rural areas of non-Western societies today. In contrast, the teenager growing up in a contemporary urban family will very likely miss out on the formative encounters such as those that Tedesse, our Ethiopian shepherd boy, experienced. They will have little opportunity to feel the thrill of exploration or the emotional solace of connection to tradition. For the Ethiopian boy living in a pastoral society such as Tedesse's, the knowledge that he is contributing to his family's well-being is an important factor in his developing self-confidence. He is earning the trust of his elders and is succeeding at a task that is important to his entire tribe; he thus has the feeling that he is carving out a place for himself within society.

Our own teenagers, for the most part, are not partners in the struggle for economic survival or success in which middle- or upper-class families are engaged. If anything, with their constant demands and desires, teenagers are experienced by their parents as a disturbance or distraction and a source of almost constant tension. More than once children have been placed in my care by their parents who, to my absolute amazement, told me that they simply don't want them around. These children were from second- or third-generation immigrant families who had sunk into impoverishment. I can still see in my mind's eye the horrifying image of an invalid parent waving his cane at his frightened child as he drove him into my office, yelling after him, "If you ever come back to our home, I'll throw you into the neighborhood garbage bin."

We know quite well that rejection in various forms—not always as direct or brutal as in the anecdote above—is not confined to families in circumstances marked by misery. The longstanding upper-class tradition of sending even small children away to boarding schools, even if the purpose was to give them a better education, evidences subterranean currents that have little in common with those stated aims. Still, teenagers can feel deep inside that they are outcasts even when remaining at home, and thus may behave accordingly. Whether the current challenge for a modern couple is succeeding in their careers or keeping their marriage alive, having a teenager underfoot is something that can often feel like an extra, unwanted load. And teenagers, with their super-sensitive emotional antennae, can feel the tension in the air. They feel the disruption that they cause within the adult world, actually experiencing it magnified as in a distorting mirror.

In contrast to Tedesse, modern teenagers do not have the freedom and the independence to explore their surroundings, to wander unimpeded through new territory. The modern urban world is too populated, too rough and dangerous, too circumscribed by private property and public laws, to allow a teenager to disappear on his own for a few weeks. Often, what is left for the child is to sink into a kind of intoxication with "things," objects that attempt to create an aura of adventure or that provide the teenager with a sense of identity and connection. These items may include clothes, movies, music, or computer games. All are ready-made for consumption and do not, in any real way, advance the teenage search for self-discovery.

Holistic Educating

Can things be otherwise? Can modern families and teenagers experience a "return to nature," in which adolescence once again becomes a true coming of age, in which a young person can discover himself while discovering the world and can find himself by learning to track his own progress on the journey of life?

This can happen only if, as parents and educators, we learn to look at our adolescents in a holistic way. In the field of health and medicine, there has been a huge movement toward healing methods that rely upon the natural healing powers inherent in each person.

In contrast to modern medicine, which has come to rely more and more on highly advanced technologies such as microsurgery and magnetic resonance imaging, natural healing methods are usually low tech and rely on processes and formulas that the patient himself can participate in executing.

One of the fascinating aspects of the Ethiopian presence in Israel is that many Ethiopians eventually make trips back to Ethiopia in order to receive health care from healers using traditional methods. This is despite the fact that in terms of modern medical science, Israel is one of the most advanced countries in the world and Ethiopia is one of the least advanced. There are just some diseases, especially chronic illnesses such as asthma, arthritis, and mental illness, which seem to respond better to traditional healing methods than to the most advanced scientific techniques. This may especially be true when, as often is the case, there is a psychosomatic element to the illness.

The most common critique that practitioners of holistic health techniques make of scientific methodologies is that they tend to focus on a particular part of the body while putting less emphasis on the way all the different parts of the body interact with each other. Oftentimes, the emotional and spiritual aspects of illness, which can be keys to the process of healing and recovery, are ignored. The strength of holistic health care lies in its emphasis on the total person, and on the way the body, mind and spirit all impact a person's physical health. If 25 years ago the medical establishment mostly looked at holistic healing as a form of fraud, today more and more hospitals and health-insurance plans recognize its efficacy and offer alternative treatments alongside mainstream therapies.

Can we transplant some of this same spirit of holism to the field of education? Educators today are armed with an array of methods and techniques that deal with learning skills and learning blocks, with fine-motor ability and attention deficit, with emotional disorders, abnormal behavior patterns and a host of other specifics. There are times when these techniques are imperative, and can make a great deal of difference in a teenager's life. But these techniques are mostly based on a fractional perspective. They focus on isolated components of a child's life. What about the child's totality? What is the total context of the child's life?

Holistic parenting and educating means returning to the most basic components of the human experience. It means understanding that the modern, urban, industrial world, rife with alienation and often bereft of community, should not be our automatic point of reference in dealing with children and adolescents. It means that as parents and educators, we have to attempt to reconstruct, in our children's lives, some of the structures of meaning, support and direction that existed for so long in human history.

GABRIEL: MORE THAN WORDS

Gabriel was an Ethiopian immigrant with a problem shared by many teenagers, although rarely with such a degree of severity. Gabriel had acne. Not just a few pimples, but an outbreak that made his whole face look like an area of volcanic activity, with mounds of angry red blemishes topped with tiny eruptions of white pus.

Compounding Gabriel's sensitivity about his appearances was the fact that during this particular time in Israel, there was a great deal of media attention being devoted to the possibility that some of the new Ethiopian immigrant population had come to Israel bearing AIDS. AIDS was known to be epidemic in some of the impoverished urban centers of East Africa. The Ethiopians, in the months preceding the Operation Solomon airlift, had spent up to a year living in conditions of squalor in Addis Ababa, where the percentage of the population carrying the AIDS virus was high.

Some of the men undoubtedly had engaged in sexual relations with women from the local population. Other members of the Beta Yisrael community were infected when they used the services of "shot doctors," traditional healers who added the hypodermic needle to their array of treatments. Many Africans have an almost supernatural belief in the power of shots because of their collective memory of their first, miraculous introduction to antibiotics. Unscrupulous and unsanitary healers take advantage of this reverence. Somehow, Gabriel connected his severe acne with AIDS. This might have had its source in the feelings of repulsion that both AIDS and his acne evoked. Or perhaps Gabriel had made some kind of subconscious association that made his acne seem leprous, like the impurity invoked by AIDS. Maybe the knowledge that AIDS can be transmitted through blood, and that his blood seemed to be "boiling" to the surface of his face, contributed to his fixation.

One fine morning, I was urgently called to the area of the water tower, where Gabriel had been caught attempting to commit suicide by leaping from the top. I brought Gabriel into my office, and learned for the first time that he was obsessed with the idea that he had been infected with AIDS. To my own astonishment, I did something that I might not have done if I had stopped to think about it with a team of psychological experts. I grabbed Gabriel's face, and began to lick his boils with my tongue, I looked him in the eyes, and said: "Would I have done that if I thought you had AIDS?" My unspoken message was more important than my verbal reassurance: If you have AIDS, my actions said, then I am willing to risk getting AIDS, too. You are not alone in the world, whatever your problems are. I am willing to share your very blood.

The story of Gabriel is an example of our holistic approach. Instead of answering Gabriel's concerns about his acne with an informative lecture about how AIDS is contracted or manifested,

I plunged in symbolically, demonstrating to him with my whole being that he did not have to be afraid. Once I allayed his fears, we could deal with how to treat his acne problem. If I had only sent him to the school nurse, his secret fears about his safety, security, and place in life would not have been addressed. Gabriel as the whole person needed my help; not just his acne.

From the moment of that encounter, Gabriel's psychological status improved. His acne eventually healed and he went on to graduate successfully from high school, to serve in the army, and to start a career in public relations and media. My response—to plunge into a repulsive act in order to demonstrate how linked I was to his agony and fear—gave Gabriel a feeling of connection that he needed with the adult world. This enabled him to continue his path towards independence. Today, he is outstanding in his capability of giving to others.

The Talmud tells us that every person is a world unto himself. Thus, "He who saves a single life, it is as if he had saved the entire world." As in Gabriel's story, there are many ways in which to save a human life. Each human being is unique and each life is of infinite value. This insight is something that we often forget in our dealings with teenagers.

ENCIRCLING IS EMBRACING

Martin Buber, one of the most acclaimed Jewish thinkers of the last century, articulated a different way to relate to other human beings—and his model has proved formative for me as an educator. Buber taught that our primary way of encountering the divine was through our relationships with other people. He said that human beings had two basic modes when relating to others: I-It and I-You. In the I-it mode, we relate to others as if they were objects. We can analyze them. We can manipulate them. We can catalogue their strengths and weaknesses, their limitations. We see them as separate from ourselves.

In the I-You mode, we encounter the totality of the other person with our whole beings. Deactivating the force field that we often use to strengthen and delineate our sense of separateness, we realize that together, through our encounter, we are both part of something new. Our meeting, if it is real, creates something that is more than the sum of each of our individual consciousnesses. In a true meeting between two individuals, the relationship is not *within* each person, but *between* them.

What is most real for Buber is the trans-individual—the spiritual world we call into being when we really face each other's uniqueness and infiniteness. We need to imbue this meeting with the full power of our will, with our own inner identity. Once we do, we are changed. During those moments of true meeting, we are part of something larger. In encountering another person we create, through our embrace, a living world of which we are both part. Buber calls this kind of meeting "encircling."

Perhaps the best way to make this idea concrete is to use an example we are all familiar with: romantic love. Lovers create a unique world that they share together, a world with its own language, geography and history. Buber's great insight is that every authentic encounter between human beings shares some of this same quality. One could say that the intentions of the people within an encounter create the laws of nature that govern the world that they together create.

When two people speak truthfully together, they create a shared world whose quality is honesty and truthfulness. When people refuse to categorize or manipulate each other in their encounters, they create a world that is not fragmented by objectifying definitions or defined by the quest for power. When people remember that the other person is unique and infinite, a world unto herself, the "laws of nature" in the world that is created are such that the totality of the other person, beyond what can be seen with the naked eye or expressed in one discrete moment, can unfold.

REAPING WHAT WE SOW

From the time I began to think of myself as an educator, these teachings became my primary source of inner guidance. Since then, I have been consumed with the question of how to apply Buber's teachings in a practical and transmittable way to interactions between people, especially during the formative period of adolescence. As educators we are entrusted with teaching our children what life is. Beyond the specific skills, concepts or languages we want them to learn, we have to teach our children something much more basic: how to be in the world, both in relation to themselves and in relation to others.

The primary way we do this is through our relationships with them. This is their lifeline, their oxygen. Essentially, what they experience coming from us is what they will be able to inhabit as a mode of being in the future. If our teenagers feel compassion and patience emanating from us as we address them and their dilemmas, they will become familiar with the world as a compassionate place and will learn to be patient and compassionate themselves. What we give to them at one stage, they will internalize and embody at the next stage. The quality of our relationship with our adolescents shapes and forms the inner structure of their worlds.

THE ADOLESCENT AS EMBRYO

Like the *Kabbalah*, the renowned psychologist Margaret Mahler, in her extensive writing on teenagers, has compared adolescence not to childhood but to a much earlier stage of development. Adolescence, she says, is like a "second birth." In biological birth, an infant is born into the circle of the immediate family. In adolescence, with biological growth moving towards completion, the child is reborn again into the social world as an embryonic adult.

One corollary of Mahler's idea of a "second birth" is that adolescence is a new start, during which traumas and wounds from childhood can be healed. Another, even more basic insight we can glean from Mahler's concept is that adolescents, no matter how independent they seem or say they want to be, are like infants who have to learn how to sit up, crawl, and stand before they can walk. If healthy adulthood is characterized by independence and individuation, Mahler's idea of a second, psychological birth in adolescence means that we have to be aware of the enormous level of support that teens need to achieve a stable adulthood.

A TUMULTUOUS AND DYNAMIC PROCESS

By imagining the teenager as an infant, we don't mean to deny the obvious teenage need for independence. This need should be respected, but should not lead us to relinquish the same profound sense of responsibility for a child's welfare that we experience when raising an infant. First and foremost, we must recognize the years of adolescence as a formative period with its own developmental stages. Over the last 100 years, theoreticians have mapped the developmental stages of infancy with great precision. No one expects an infant to walk before it can stand, or to speak before it can walk. And although the crying of a six-month old can be annoying, to say the least, the vast majority of us are wise enough not to yell at or strike an infant as punishment for crying.

As educators, we must internalize the fact that the adolescent journey to adulthood works itself out through a developmental path, and that the different forms of acting out and rebelliousness that our teens display are in no way representative of the final configuration their personalities and behaviors will form. Our teenagers are works in progress, living through a tumultuous and dynamic process. We must remain constantly aware of this fact in our hearts and minds.

IMAGES AS WORKING TOOLS

In order to create a working tool for our educators, who are constantly dealing with children from broken homes and broken worlds, we have created within the Yemin Orde Youth Village our own catalogue of images. These images represent the ideas that form the core of our educational philosophy, and include the two circles introduced earlier—the circle of *Tikkun Olam* (mending the world) and the circle of *Tikkun HaLev* (mending the heart). We had previously described the two circles as tools for broadening the conceptual horizon of our work as educators to include an awareness of human history and contemporary society; for focusing us on the deep and often unconscious emotional struggles of adolescence; and for better understanding the interrelationship between these realms. Now we see that the image of the circle is not only an image of awareness, but of connection. The circle symbolizes the shared world we create in our relationships with our teenagers, and the existential bond that links us together in our role as mentors.

Can we defy the conventional wisdom of our era, in regards to raising children and adolescents, in order to create the aura of togetherness they need? Starting as far back as Dr. Spock's famous *Baby and Child Care*, first published in the early 1960s, we have been told that if we are too supportive of our children we will create dependency in them. Especially in the United States and other places influenced by this ethos of self-reliance, the message we have been conditioned to send to our teenagers is, "We may be taking care of your needs right now, but soon enough, you'll be out there on your own. And then? You had better be strong, because it's sink or swim."

Isn't this the wrong message to give? True, we have to help our children grow wings that will allow them to fly. However, the way to accomplish this is not through messages that magnify the sense of fracturedness and shattering already so characteristic of modernity.

One prevailing response to disciplinary problems, used almost instinctually by both schools and parents, is to invoke the threat of abandonment and separation. If a teenager is acting out—which most healthy teens will, to one extent or another—many parents will threaten him with some form of "shape up or ship out." This might mean telling the adolescent that he will be sent to boarding school or some kind of quasi-military summer camp if he cannot abide by the rules of the house. In educational settings, the threat might be expulsion, a tactic developed in order to foster excellence and create elite groups by "weeding out" disrupters. In both cases, disapproval is conveyed through a withholding or severing of emotional connections.

Yet what these tactics do is to merge, within the teenager's mind and experience, rebellion and the threat of abandonment. Since rebellion is one of the teenagers' main tools for testing their strength and independence, this strategy actually serves to hurt a teen's development towards healthy independence. One possible outcome is that the teenager will curtail his rebellious instincts because of an anxiety over separation, thus leaving the feelings originally expressed by acting out smoldering and unresolved. Another possibility is that a teenager's rebellion will be fueled by the perceived cruelty of a world whose code of justice is based on the threat of abandonment.

In general, the cult of independence is closely connected to the modern capitalist ethic that mythologizes the idea of "the self-made man" who has "pulled himself up by his own bootstraps" (try it—it happens to be impossible) and made it without help from others. With all due respect to the amazing accomplishments of capitalism, no human being ever makes it in the world without help. I have sometimes had occasion to see what I consider to be the psychological results of the current orthodoxy of the American myth of self-reliance. Typically, successful, workaholic fathers will attempt to foster independence in their children when they are in their late teens or twenties. "Now you're going to have to make it on your own," they tell their sons or daughters. Sometimes they will give them some money and send them away to another city, state or country. They believe that by having their children make their own way in the world they will increase their self-confidence and strength.

Hard work is very important. But in these cases, parents' unstated—but clearly heard—message to their children is not about the value of hard work. It is that we are living in a dog-eat-dog, every-man-for-himself world; a world in which children cannot rely on parents. Children reared in this type of atmosphere may express pride in their parents and the efforts they have made to make it on their own. But beneath the surface, their voices tell another story. Children of successful parents who have demanded that they "make it on their own" often betray woundedness and lack true inner confidence. Even if they have become successful, these children often are not emotionally secure and happy.

The irony, of course, is that the first generation of successful businessmen have often hailed from more traditional homes, where immigrant parents provided a potent model of emotional commitment to children. Their nearly penniless fathers would never have given them a few dollars and told them to scram, as they did to their own sons. And so they took the strength of their father's love and unconditional commitment with them into the business world or professional world, and were enormously successful. But their own children, the third generation, became victims of the gospel of self-reliance applied in a misguided way, and never really achieved the kind of emotional self-confidence that would allow them to radiate the power and independence that their parents did.

But aren't we responsible for teaching our children how to survive? Of course we are. However, the sink-or-swim school of building confidence in life is founded on a basic misconception. Human beings by nature are not parasites that must be forcibly weaned from a natural preference towards dependency. Teenagers *want* to become independent. They want a place in the world, an identity they can call their own. They want to become active, honored contributors to society. They want to arrive at the stage when they can make their own decisions, trust their own judgment, and have the power to navigate in the directions they choose. Like plants, which grow in the direction of sunlight, the natural tendency of teenagers is to be attracted to independence.

But plants, in order to grow towards the sunlight, need soil and water as well as sun. And among the nutrients that children need in order to develop towards independence is confidence in the future. They need exactly the kind of confidence that is undermined by questions such as, "What will you do when I am no longer here?" or statements like, "When you are 18, you're out of the house and on your own." This kind of message amplifies the threat of an already threatening world. Instead of encouraging our teens to make for the open seas, the threat of loneliness, separation, and failure will send them scurrying for safe shores. Our anxiety over the possibility of future dependency will inevitably be internalized by our teens as a fear of the world, fear of the future, or lack of confidence in their abilities.

It may sound paradoxical, but the real message teens need in order to move towards independence is, "I'm with you now and I will be with you in the future. I will do everything in my power to make sure that your life is successful." This is the embrace, the shared circle of fates that our embryonic adults need from us. If our teens feel our embrace, they will be able to internalize us, to carry us around with them into the future, as a source of confidence and strength. And, through the world we create together, they can learn that the larger world "out there" is not composed of separation and loneliness alone, but also of warmth, togetherness and commitment to each other. This can only happen if we keep intact our capacity to connect with this simple truth, which challenges much of what passes for wisdom in today's world.

Assuming Normalcy

Every September for the past 30 years, hundreds of teenagers begin another year of their lives on our mountain at Yemin Orde. Every day, 365 days a year, 24 hours a day, the stream of life continues here. Still, the start of the new school year, along with the Jewish High Holy Days, marks the lives of the teenagers; a new year is a new start. Every school year we are confronted with the need to integrate new educators, in particular counselors, into our staff. Counselors are usually young men and women in their early twenties—often just finished with their mandatory army service and some of them Yemin Orde graduates themselves—who are on the front lines of our village's educational endeavor. Each counselor is charged with supervising the daily life of a specific group of youngsters who live together in one of our many houses. They often are the ones who have to deal in real time with the nearly constant flood of tiny crises, blow-ups, and emotional oscillations that characterize adolescent life. Because of the pressure and intensity of their task, combined with their relative youth, counselors often experience emotional "burn out"—thus the relatively high turnover rate that translates into a continuous need for training seminars.

Every new school year thus confronts us with a crucial and perplexing question: Is it possible to almost instantly transform these young educators for the work they will be doing with our teenagers? How can one distill experience into a language that is not just theoretical, but practical, flexible and effective enough for the shifting circumstances of day-to-day life in the village?

This question, in one form or another, has been asked ad-infinitum over the past 100 years. An explosion of guidebooks for parents written by "experts" of various kinds has attempted to answer it. At least once every decade, trends and ideas have changed and a new generation of child-rearing books has gained favor. Sometimes it seems as if the plethora of guidebooks is actually a direct indication of the diminution of parental confidence, a retreat from the natural relationship between parent and child to be found in more traditional societies.

One sign of this retreat is the prevalence of psychological language and concepts in the modern discourse on child-rearing. Is the goal to supply us with this specialized knowledge so that we can replace psychologists in the therapeutic role? The answer is obviously no. A person who has not trained as a psychologist, under expert supervision over a relatively long period of internship, should not assume that he has become one by reading a book. Psychology should be left to psychologists, who should be utilized only in cases that suggest pathology. Psychological therapy takes place in a special environment, one step removed from everyday life. But as educators, we need a way to navigate the natural flow of life we share with our children.

The psychotherapeutic terminology that has become part of common parlance can also help us clarify the difference between the kind of help therapy offers and the kind of involvement in children's lives we are advocating for educators. In psychotherapy, "containment" is a central motif. The growing prevalence of "psychological" call-in radio and television programs and popular paperback "how-to" books, people today speak about "containing" each other as if it were a natural mode of relating to other people.

Ideally, in the process of containment the therapist empties himself of his own concerns, and turns himself totally to the task of listening, leading the client towards new insights about himself. The notion of containment may have its place within the specialized context of therapy, with its intensely focused fifty-minute slots of time. Yet, in everyday life, is "containment" a realistic option?

Rather than containing our teenagers we should strive to encircle them, which as Buber's thinking suggests, comes as naturally to us as an embrace. Our goal should be to produce a shared circle that marks the boundaries of our shared fate, rather than a containment that reeks of a built-in hierarchical relationship in which one side has all the enlightenment and the other side all the pain and confusion.

Containment also is something that is nearly impossible to carry off during the course of everyday life, at those odd and often stressful moments when teachers encounter children. One of my close friends is a child psychologist. It always fascinates and amuses me to see how he is with his own children—no different from the rest of us, sometimes losing patience, and certainly never engaging in the kind of thinking and behavior he does when doing therapy.

What we are interested in is bringing ourselves to our children "as is," in the midst of life. Our emphasis is not on seeing the pathological, abnormal side of adolescence. It is normality we want to focus on. Hasn't the time arrived for us to reassess and broaden our notion of what is normal? If we assume that our teenagers are normal, and that their behavior, though challenging, makes sense within the context of their journey to adulthood, doesn't that stand a good chance of becoming a self-fulfilling prophecy?

7

EDUCATION EMANATING FROM BODY AND SOUL

Perhaps the main problem with the cascade of guidebooks that have filled educators' and parents' shelves over the last hundred years is that in their attempts to prescribe strategies and behaviors they have in fact contributed to a more technocratic approach. This approach weakens the natural flow of relationships between educators/parents and children and diverts them in undesirable directions. Our goal is not to provide adults with yet another guidebook, or techniques to fill their toolkit, but instead to help them find a place to stand so that in day-to-day encounters they themselves can serve as guides for their teens en route to a healthy and independent adulthood. For each of us, whatever our history and beliefs, it is *our* past, *our* values, *our* strengths—and our ability to hold our children's developmental path within our mind's eye, which we must bring to educating children.

Every new year in training and retraining our staff, we aspire to introduce the utmost clarity into the process of identifying the basic structure of the world that we have to convey to our children if they are to feel secure in their journey. The physical embrace that is a natural part of our response to children can be transformed through a language of symbols and graphic expressions into a way of relating to the world of the adolescent that is a practical translation of Buber's concept of "encirclement"—the existential dimension of the circles of *Tikkun Olam* and *Tikkun HaLev*.

The trick, however, is to make the images real—so real that you can feel them in your body. "Stand up and stretch out your arms," I say to a group of young counselors as a new year begins, an effort to transmit the language and images that can activate the potency and applicability that theoretical knowledge lacks. I wish them to feel their power to educate, physically and mentally. In this attempt I have discovered for myself the principle expounded in George B. Leonard's book *Education and Ecstasy*—namely that all true educational paths have a foundation in ecstatic experience.

"Imagine that your left arm is stretched out so far that it is touching the past, so that its metaphoric weight is resting on your palm, as if your source is all there: ancestors, culture, memories," I say to them. "Now turn your head and watch your other arm until your eyes reach your palm, where the metaphoric weight of your future rests. Close your eyes, and feel time flowing from one outstretched palm to the other, the past moving through you towards the future. Feel the weight of your presence, your center. Slowly pull the past and the future toward yourself, towards the center. Feel how solidly your feet are standing on the earth, feel your full presence. Now lift your attention upward, toward the sky, toward the infinite. Let your inner voice remind you of your highest aspirations and beliefs."

After reviewing numerous educational and psychological theories it is important to me that our staff feel that education emanates primarily from our specificity and our depth—from body and soul, from our center of gravity. This is, after all, what each of our adolescents is seeking in us.

Ultimately, to hone this inner sense of sharpened relevance in our children's world, we move to the next step: Feeling how the lines that define our being are set within the two concentric circles.

"Turn around one full revolution," I suggest. "Feel the limits of your being. Imagine two concentric circles defining this limit. Sense the circle closest to yourself, immediately surrounding you, defining and enclosing your existential experience. Now imagine the circle farthest away, the outer boundary of where your awareness reaches. Can you feel these circles defining for you a platform within the infinite? Can they also represent the space into which each of us can grow?"

When we find our center of gravity within these two circles, the circle of *Tikkun HaLev* and the circle of *Tikkun Olam,* our sense of presence is activated. We radiate the inner quality of genuine wholeness. This priceless moment of insight is the cornerstone of our transformation as mentors.

Over the years I have become convinced that this exercise, and the conceptual world that informs it, have helped us locate the archetypal "village" that defines human hopes and have enabled us to infuse the Yemin Orde Village with its almost utopian quality. This has made our village a place in which both staff and teenagers can cope with tensions, outbursts and differences of opinion without needing to shatter and shock. This simple exercise, absorbed and internalized, can charge the air in which the relationship between adults and teenagers is transpiring with positive electrolytes, by serving as a basic outline inside of which the contents of our life experience can adhere. It is a mnemonic device that reminds me how to fill my relationship with a teenage child with emotional content, so that I am not perceived as absent or as one-dimensional.

INVOKING WHOLENESS

The effort to internalize the basic framework of circles and lines, to carry it around with us as a language of images, is reminiscent of the spiritual and ritual attempt to symbolize cosmic wholeness. Religions such as Hinduism and Buddhism have *mandala*s, complex, semi-abstract circular pictures that are representations of the cosmos in its totality. Judaism has rituals like the waving of the *lulav* (palm fronds) and *etrog* (citron) during the Festival of Tabernacles (*Sukkot*), in which one stands centered on a single point and gestures in all directions: north, east, south, west, up and down.

Other ancient civilizations similarly understood the universe and all within it, including biological processes and human temperament, as being comprised of a small number of basic elements. These differed in number and kind, but equally contributed to the evolution of a discourse about the basic foundational structure of the universe. Although modern science has moved us a few steps beyond ancient times, we still speak about basic elements—solids, liquids, gases, and energy—in describing the universe. The idea of basic elements has thus been an important conceptual tool that has allowed people to talk about deep, underlying structures of reality that otherwise might remain hidden from view. It enables us to simplify and de-mystify confusing details and unexplained phenomena in order to more clearly mark the borders of our awareness.

MENU OF THEMES

In the same way, by utilizing symbols that make vivid for us the basic parameters of our own world and that of the adolescent, we have a better chance of perceiving him or her in a holistic fashion. I still remember the special 3D-glasses that were a fad in the 1950s and early 1960s (and are now making a comeback). Handed out before certain movies, they were supposed to make the flat film screen seem as if it were three dimensional. I'm not sure those glasses worked very well, but they make an apt metaphor for what the framework of circles and lines can do. It can give us a completely new perspective on our teenagers by creating a kind of three-dimensional perception within our mind and heart. The fundamental elements it describes quickly remind us of the total context of a teenager's life—of the journey they are on, and of the emotional depths within them. We can carry this picture of the two lines surrounded by two circles with us in our minds; they are the 3D glasses that we can slip on as we interact with our teenagers. At the same time as they help us locate our own center, the two lines and two circles also focus us on our teenagers, placing them right at the center of our vision.

Unlike the 3D glasses, our framework is a tool for looking both inside and outside ourselves. When we feel ourselves anchored in past and present, in earth and sky, we appear to our children as an Archimedean point of gravity in the face of the tides of chaos. Friedrich Nietzsche observed that in the Hebrew language the words for honor and for weight share the same root letters. The Hebrew word *kavod* in the Bible refers to a kind of radiance emanating from the divine as from other entities or personalities that possess integrity and a realized identity. Cultivating a kind of awareness filtered through the circles and lines can help us achieve the kind of center of gravity we need in order to transmit a sense of weight, rootedness and honor to our children.

Without its defining contours and vectors, a person's sense of self can seem like a tiny point of consciousness. Alone against a vast horizon, always in danger of being swept away by the tides of the infinite, tumultuous world, such a threatened consciousness is incapable of absorbing the rainbow colors of experience into his inner self. By anchoring ourselves in the past and future, represented by the horizontal line, and by paying close attention to the earth we are standing upon while aspiring to the heights represented by the vertical line, our sense of self expands. The place these two lines meet is the center of our being from which we expand towards the circles of meaning and association that enclose us. We no longer experience our consciousness as a small point adrift in a great sea.

The lines that run between past and future and between earth and sky, along with the two concentric circles that surround them do not only help us find our own center of gravity. They also provide us with the overall blueprint for the contents that should fill our relationships with teenagers. They function like chapter headings, like a menu of themes whose presence in our lives makes all the difference. No week with our teens should go by without us touching, one way or another, on these contents. Much of the rest of what follows will suggest how our newly found awareness can bring the presence of these elements into our shared lives.

EARTH AND SKY, PAST AND FUTURE

The center point of the circles, where the horizontal and vertical lines meet, is our psychological present; the very particular moment in which we interact with our children and in which we experience reality. This center point is the immediate environment, the current space-time coordinate in which we are alive. The present is the most fluid of the elements because it is constantly in formation and is subject to all the stimuli and variables of the ever-changing kaleidoscope we call life, from the weather to the current emotional and physical state of each person. In fact, because existential time, the time of the present, *is* so fluid, and because we have so little control of what is going to happen to us at every particular moment, we arrange the elements in our consciousness so that the present is constantly in the center, whatever we are doing. The other elements, which we keep touching and reinforcing, are anchors that serve to affix a sense of stability to the present moment. Touching these elements can provide for our children a meaningful and reassuring context. They also remind us of the total situation of their life so that we are not harmfully distracted by the emotions and attitudes they throw in our face at any given moment.

Representing movement from the past, from where we have already been, towards the future, where we are going, the horizontal line thus marks the principal vector of the adolescent's journey, which like our own, is a journey through time. The vertical line begins in the existential present, at the center between past and future—"earth"—and it extends upwards towards a transcendent horizon that is beyond time—"sky." "Earth" represents the actual reality; the environment, emotional surroundings, and conditions of adolescents' existential present. It is, so to speak, that which is closest to them, the ground below their feet.

And we must pay attention to this ground. With all their defiant desire for independence, teenagers still want to be mothered. They want us to notice if they are hungry, cold or tired, if their room is a mess, or if they need immediate physical or emotional help. Through our gentle, non-intrusive attention to their "earth" dimension, we can demonstrate our embrace of them. We are often concerned that if we respond too generously to our children's constant demands, we will "spoil" them. And certainly, teenagers should be encouraged to take a large share of responsibility in tending to their own needs and pitching in on household chores. But what we call "spoiling"—an overdeveloped anxiety about one's immediate environment and an inability to delay gratification—is usually learned from the parents/mentors themselves. Since children internalize and embody our attitudes towards them, when we are able to wholeheartedly gesture our love and care by responding to our children's needs we are likely to be rewarded with goodhearted children who are attentive to the needs of others.

To be aware of the earth element, which is the center point of our diagram, means to focus in on the details of the particular moment. What are the pressures, both physical and psychological, that are affecting adolescents at this particular moment in their life?

Being aware of the earth point means also being aware of one's own current situation. Are *you* tired, aloof, disappointed, angry, or even hungry? How is your physical or emotional state affecting your responses to your child? Notice this, and adjust accordingly. Or at the very least, don't blame your children for what is going on inside of you. Try not to allow yourself to be swept away from your task of awareness by your shifting moods or needs. While it may seem inconceivable to take all of what is going on within yourself into account in real time when facing your child, the flashing symbol of the lines and the circles can be like igniting a flame in order to illuminate a dark cavern.

The vertical line points from earth upwards, toward the transcendent—toward the ideas and ideals that guide our lives. They may be guiding ideals such as justice, peace or love of humanity, or they me be love of God and obedience to religious teachings. Whatever their form, ideals will always be an important component of a wholesome life. An idealistic drive is one of the primary characteristics of adolescents, and if we are to be part of their world, we need to recognize this. Part of what we have to do as parents or educators is to clarify the ideals that are important to us. Our ideals may have faded; raising teens challenges us to polish them up. By presenting our ideals to our teenagers—not in the form of a fiat, but in a way that will nourish teenage idealism—we can help them express their own idealistic drive. Teenagers will often reject the ideals we share with them. For many teenagers, this is almost necessary if they are eventually to embrace them as their own. This should not faze us. Ultimately, years later, our children may surprise us by returning to the values they once decisively rejected. Our job is not to lock teenagers into specific ideals, but rather to show them a universe in which ideals matter.

These are the four elements, then, that define our two lines: one running from past to future, the second rising from earth towards the sky. The past, again, is adolescents' own past, their childhood and all that that entails, and their collective past, the past of their family and culture. The future is both their own future, which is already alive in their imagination and heart as the destination and the source of their future identity, and the future of the world in which they will live. The earth is the ground on which they stand, everything that makes up his day-to-day physical and emotional environment. And the sky is the ideals that fire their ethical imagination, and the ideas that help them understand their place in the larger scheme of things.

THE AWARENESS OF BROKENNESS IS ITSELF WHOLENESS

The two circles have names taken from Jewish philosophy and mysticism. Both names begin with the word *tikkun,* which means to mend or repair. The concept of *tikkun* is central to the Jewish notion that human beings are partners with God. God left creation in an imperfect state in order to allow us to play a role in transforming the world and making it whole. The two circles—one of which represents the inner realm of the individual human heart, while the other indicates our reaching out to the widening circle of mankind—are representations of wholeness and of the unending process of attempting to reach that wholeness. The circles create boundaries; they thus represent the impossibility of reaching the unbounded whole, the complete, for who can completely heal themselves or the world? But the circle, which mathematicians call the perfect form, also means that the part that you are doing has a quality of wholeness. We are always dealing with the world of brokenness, but our very willingness to face and touch and try to heal this brokenness in ourselves and in others is in itself whole. In the words of one of the Hasidic sages, "There is nothing as whole as a broken heart." The awareness of brokenness is itself wholeness.

The moment that you as an educator realize that within the inner world of your child there are uncharted depths, things that are hidden from you and also from him or her, you have touched wholeness. Adolescents, as they search to define their identity, struggle with many dualities that seem to have a life of their own within their questioning consciousness. Am I strong or weak? Good or bad? Attractive or repulsive? A success or a failure? Parents must learn to recognize the presence of duality, and understand that each pair of opposites is joined at the root of their teenager's consciousness, like the two sides of a coin.

Too often, parents are locked into either a hypercritical mode or a discourse that allows mostly for sweet praise and positive reinforcement. While it is easy to understand the destructive nature of constant criticism, merely giving positive reinforcement without being aware of the other side of the coin will also ultimately boomerang, building up children's suspicions of a lack of authenticity and ultimately polluting the dialogue and interaction between adults and children.

The circle of *Tikkun HaLev* is all about balancing between dualities, helping us to recognize the wholeness they in fact create within our child and within us. It also helps us to recognize the subconscious depths that lie below the level of immediate, existential awareness. These are also part of the adolescent mind, as they are part of our own psyche. Our awareness of the circle of *Tikkun HaLev* advises us that the journey to adulthood is a journey towards integration and healing, in which dualities synergistically integrate into a greater whole.

SPIRALS OF INSIGHT AND TRANSFORMATION

The circle of *Tikkun HaLev* represents insight; the ability to learn from the suffering we have endured and the mistakes we have made through inner reflection. Why a circle? Because insight is produced when a new experience touches an old one—a memory, wound or a blind spot—and we suddenly understand, and are illuminated. The seemingly unrelenting forward movement of our existence in time, represented by the horizontal line stretching from past to future, actually loops back upon itself when we gain insight. Later events, through their parallels and similarities, shed light on earlier ones. Our experiences as we move through the straight line of time can seem arbitrary; when time becomes a circle, we see the contours of a story, of our story. The circle thus surrounds and protects us by allowing us to feel that life, despite its relentless rush forward, has meaning.

The flow of the year through the seasons is another way in which the circular aspect of time is revealed. Religious and secular holidays are marked at exactly the same point every year, and every week in Yemin Orde, as in other Jewish communities, a section of the *Torah* is read and discussed. In this fashion, the Five Books of Moses are read each year in their entirety. On *Simchat Torah*, the last day of the fall Festival of Tabernacles, the last words of the Torah are read—and immediately Genesis is begun again. Commentators throughout the generations have noted that when the last letter of the *Torah* is connected to the first letter of the *Torah*, the letters spell *Lev*, or heart. The heart gains knowledge as we allow the same teachings to touch and penetrate the new experiences we have celebrated or suffered during the year. The linear course of time is thus encircled with insight.

TORAPY—BEDTIME STORIES FOR THE WOUNDED HEART

The disturbing aspects of day to day life hit adolescents with a primal force to which adults have largely become inured. One vital insight that all great literary traditions can impart upon teenagers is that they are not alone in their agonizing quandaries. The dualistic structure of adolescent thought means that teens tend to split reality into categories of good and evil, purity and defilement; when these categories collapse, the conclusions they draw are often harsh and disturbing. When a teenager witnesses disharmony in the family, unfaithfulness, or dishonesty; when she is disappointed by a trusted someone, or herself, she often will experience overwhelming feelings of brokenness and heartbreak. The world seems dark, and her existential state *is* one of inconsolable grief. A teenager's despair is heightened by a sense of being utterly alone in her knowledge and situation, as if she were unique in perceiving the falseness and tragedy that permeates the world.

Bedtime stories ease the fears of young children as they travel towards the unknown of night and sleep. They renew children's emotional connection with their parents even as they provide the children with a language that articulates and interprets their fears. During the teenage years, great works of literature can play the role that bedtime stories did during early childhood—addressing unspoken fears and strengthening intergenerational connections. Especially when mediated by adult mentors, stories from the great literary traditions can ease the sting of this loneliness, transforming what teenagers thought they were carrying in solitude into part of the human condition, and thus opening up a space for dialogue and integration. In our village, I use the Book of Books, the Torah, whose pedigree of ancientness and sacredness is for us unsurpassed. Half jokingly, I call the weekly themes with which I flood the Village consciousness Torapy, Torah messages that are aimed at the wounded, growing heart.

As often as possible, I will try to touch on the primal conflicts, contradictions and dilemmas so prevalent in the biblical narrative: brother killing brother, drunkenness as an escape and humiliation, fathers sacrificing sons, sexual misadventures, jealousy between sisters and so on. By being as sharp, even as outrageous as possible, I hope to bring to the surface adolescent obsessions whose repression drains psychic energy.

"King David took a married woman!" I might exclaim, hoping to open the closed subject of marital betrayals and ruined families that many children in our village and elsewhere carry as a secret burden. I might shout, in our weekly discussion, "How could a father sell his son?" in reference to Reuben's promise to his father Jacob—knowing full well that many of the children in the village feel, to varying degrees, that they have been abandoned by their parents. By linking such painful themes to the narrative of the Torah, I convey to them a broader context of sanctity and wholesomeness. By emphasizing the way in which even the greatest of biblical heroes struggled with potentially devastating flaws and temptations, I hope to ameliorate the paralyzing effect which evidence of weakness and corruption often has on teenage minds.

Through Torapy we wish ultimately to convey the message that brokenness and wholeness can coexist in our world, and that the dualities that haunt teenagers bear the possibility of integration. For example, in Genesis, God instructs Abraham to seal their covenant by splitting the bodies of three sacrificial animals, and walking between them, while leaving the body of a sacrificial bird whole. I tease out the symbolism of this story, emphasizing the bird left whole as the ultimate vision of wholeness and unification whose imprint remains before us even as we journey through an often broken and fragmented reality. We repeat the phrase "And the bird was not divided" over and over again during the week of its Torah portion, posted on the bulletin board, and mentioned on our community television broadcasts, until it is lodged in the memory of the teens to take with them through life. Whenever they recall that phrase, they will recall a cluster of associations about brokenness and wholeness, reality and radical hope.

My hope is that our children take at least one provocative phrase from each of the fifty-odd weekly Torah portions with them on their journey through life. This cycle of ideas and phrases are like doors through which they can enter a system that has its own inner logic and wholeness. I sometimes call these phrases mantras, because our intention is that, through repetition, they become absorbed into the subconscious, emerging into the conscious mind when necessary. In a sense, though, they are the opposite of mantras. Instead of a hypnotic, meditative effect, I want these phrases to catalyze critical thinking, to remind our youngsters of the larger frameworks of life beyond their immediate situations, and to locate them within the intergenerational web across which living wisdom is transmitted.

On at least one occasion, one of our graduates has told me how a Torapy phrase literally saved two lives. Fassil, an Ethiopian youngster, had the bad luck of falling under the command of an abusive officer during basic training. This officer was apparently threatened by Fassil's blackness; in any event, he took advantage of every occasion he could to remind Fassil that he was "primitive" and racially and culturally different. "When he shamed me in front of my whole platoon, I could feel the blood rushing to my head. I felt myself losing control, about to turn my automatic rifle on him, I was so furious. Then I remembered what you had taught us, "Ta'ala be'idn S'gid Leh." It is a quotation, in Aramaic, from the Talmud that explains why Jacob bowed before his own son Joseph, and means "the fox will speak in its time," or "every dog has his day." Fassil said, "I was suddenly able to look at my officer as a dog having his day. And I knew that I would have my day as well. I felt my hand, which had begun to tighten around my weapon, relax."

On another occasion, in a phone call out of the blue from another army officer, who sounded puzzled and bemused, I heard the following story: "Shai, who I understand is one of your former charges, is on trial at our base for disobedience. I'm his judge, and he told me that if I want to understand him, I should call you and say the code words "Vayigash Eilav Yehuda.'" I knew immediately what Shai meant. Those three words, which mean "And Judah approached him," describe Judah's lion-hearted decision to confront the Egyptian viceroy who has arrested his brother Benjamin. Judah still does not know that the viceroy is actually his long lost brother Joseph. Because of this scene, conveyed by these three words, Judah has become our symbol of the moral power of the individual confronting authority with courage. What had happened was that Shai had been assigned kitchen duty, and had seen how the army kitchen threw out enormous quantities of bread each day. In our Village, we had always preached that throwing away bread when there are hungry people in the world is a sin. Shai had gone on strike, refusing to take part in training until the army found a way to get the bread to those who needed it. "You have a Judah on your hands," I told his officer.

Shai was tried and put on probation for disobedience—but the incident was left off his record. Later, Shai's officer told him: "You're made of the same stuff as leaders."

FIXING YOUR ALL

The psychological healing that accompanies a successful journey from adolescence to adulthood cannot take place in isolation. Through Torapy, we connect *Tikkun HaLev* with an ancient tradition whose major focus is the transformation of the world. This is the outer circle of *Tikkun Olam*. A central component of Yemin Orde's message is that we are all part of something larger than ourselves, part of a human community that needs us just as we need it. Our self-definition and our healing is part of a process leading toward *Tikkun Olam*, the fixing of the world. In Jewish philosophy, the trajectory of human history is leading toward a messianic time, envisioned by the prophets, in which violence and corruption will cease, and knowledge, peace and brotherhood will fill the earth.

Gershom Scholem, one of the preeminent academic scholars of Judaism of the 20th century and a friend and contemporary of Martin Buber, pointed out that the Jewish concept of Messianic redemption differs from the Christian concept in at least one important way. For Christians, who believe that the messiah has already come, a person can experience messianic redemption through their relationship with Jesus, regardless of the current state of the world. In Jewish tradition, messianic redemption means the transformation of the physical, concrete world. Personal redemption cannot be disconnected from the redemption of all of life. There exists a profound relationship between a person's own individual spiritual development and their efforts to "bring the Messiah"—to catalyze the transformation of humanity for which we are all waiting.

A Hassidic master, called the *Alexander Rebbe* after the Polish town in which he lived, expressed this relationship succinctly. He said that a person is comprised of many different parts, but also has an "all," a totality that is more than the sum of their parts. It is possible to purify and fix all the different parts of oneself in isolation from others, the Rabbi of Alexander said. But if you want to fix your "all," your wholeness, the totality of yourself, you have to be engaged in bringing the Messiah, in working for *Tikkun Olam*. The two concentric circles represent this relationship. *Tikkun HaLev* widens into *Tikkun Olam*. And the reverse is true as well. Learning to identify and connect with the pain of others is a key part of *Tikkun Olam*; by healing the loneliness that is at the heart of many of our wounds, it is thus a catalyst of *Tikkun HaLev*.

On a simpler level, we can understand the relationship between the two *Tikkuns* by returning to our traditional village. Ultimately, the journey to adulthood in a traditional village means a journey to a position of respect and honor within the community. To be a respected adult means to have acquired wisdom of the kind that is used to solve disputes between neighbors, to make peace between man and wife, and to negotiate good relations between rival tribes. Human beings are communal by nature, and there is a deep and significant relationship between self-fulfillment and the kind of communal responsibility that we can identify as the drive towards *Tikkun Olam*.

The circle of *Tikkun Olam* binds us together with our children in our shared quest for a better world. It reminds us that the very act of parenting or educating is part of that quest. Parents do not choose the children they have been given, and their children are not meant to be young clones that will realize their parent's unfulfilled ambitions or assuage their parent's egos with their accomplishments. Likewise, educators often have little choice in the children who become their charges. Sound mentoring and parenting means realizing that the responsibility of raising children to a happy, healthy and productive adulthood is part of *Tikkun Olam*. An essential part of the healthy adulthood we are raising them towards is one in which the drive towards *Tikkun Olam* is legitimized and strengthened.

HEIGHTS AND DEPTHS WITHIN OUR TEENAGERS

Relationships with teenagers that are defined by the exercise of one-sided authority are toxic. So is the other extreme, reneging on all hierarchy and the responsibility of guidance. So how can we balance between these two extremes of the pendulum?

Life is a never-ending journey, but in relation to our teenagers we must also recognize our role as people who have, to a certain extent, already arrived. Whether we feel up to it or not, we are role models for our children. The need for adult models is so deep in children and teens that scientists may someday discover that it is genetic. From the materials we give them, our children must forge a model of adulthood that they can take with them internally on their journey through life. And in a deeper sense, they must learn about themselves and about the world through us, through the universe we forge in our relationship.

Our framework of lines and circles can help us play a significant part in our children's lives without conceiving this role in terms of hierarchy or control, and allow us to conceptualize our children's life as a totality. The symbolic language we use can help us understand that whatever aspect of themselves our teens are revealing at a given moment is only a partial expression of who they are—only one part of a duality that they contain within themselves. This is one of the important insights we have to keep in mind concerning teenagers. They can be one thing one moment, and something completely different the next. Like a deep-sea fisherman, they keep pulling personas out from the depths of their subconscious, trying them out, throwing them back into the waters. We have to show them consistency in our willingness to be patient and loving, without demanding from them a consistency that is just not yet part of who they are.

In order to use the symbolic language of the lines and the circles in our relationship with our teens, we have to raise our mentoring to another level of awareness. Our consciousness of our task, our ability to *intend* in our relationship to our children, is the greatest resource we have. It is the extra value added that can transform our ability to educate.

A River Flowing from Eden

The nature and quality of an educator's intention is something that adolescents instantly absorb. People often underestimate the ability of children in general and adolescents in particular to interpret non-verbal signals; to understand, in an intuitive but precise way, the emotions that precede and accompany our words.

Jewish mysticism places a great deal of emphasis on the idea of *kol,* or voice, as opposed to *dibbur,* or words. While the tongue, palate, lips and teeth create the particular sounds of each individual word, the voice emanates from deeper inside of us, from the region of our lungs and heart. Teenagers are sensitive to the source of that emanation. Our voice carries our emotions, whether we want to reveal how we feel or not. Teens will instantly be able to tell if the voice addressing them is emerging from a heart of stone or crumbling earth—filled with fear, distraction or impatience—or emanating like a living spring from a place of empathy, focus, and concern. Teenagers listen more to certain adults because they reveal something confidence-inspiring or trustworthy from their inner depths when they speak. Their voices are full, rather than hollow.

If we think of every sentence we speak as the lyrics of a song, then the voice is like the melody that colors and carries the words to our hearts. It may happen that a youngster approaches me at a moment in which I am focused on something else. The computer is crashing, I'm late for a meeting, and three key staff members have called in sick. All of us know these situations well. How do I answer this request, which may be presented with great urgency, but to an incidental observer might seem trivial? The split second before I respond is of critical importance. Overwhelmed as I am, the easiest thing would be to answer in a technical fashion, telling the young person quickly and tersely that this is not the right time or that I am not the right person to answer them. But once I have consciously trained myself, until it is second nature, to visualize within myself a reflection of the adolescent's world—a world that includes emotional depths—I can respond in a split second from the depths of my own self, and from there create a line of communication untainted by tension.

In conveying to teenagers that what concerns them also really concerns me, even if I can't deal with it immediately, my choice of words is not as important as my intonation and the look in my eyes. In the long run, this teenager will learn that delay is not rejection, and that credibility need not be measured only in terms of immediate availability. The lines and circles, by helping us focus our attention and our intention, can give us that extra moment of concentration that lifts our response out of the realm of the tense order of daily life. Speaking from the place within us that lies at the center of the circles, where the lines meet, can transform our response from anger, threat and defensiveness into voice and action emanating from an undamaged place within us.

Along with our voice, we should be conscious of our body language when we are with our adolescents. The way we stand and move and the quality of our touch can subtly shift our relationship with our teenagers to convey strength, grace, and warmth. Even when we shake a child's hand, it is possible for our touch to linger a heartbeat longer. Educating is a routine of breaking conventions. When we look into our adolescent's eyes, can we feel assurance pouring from our own eyes towards theirs? Perhaps childhood is so often remembered as a kind of Eden because people often speak to children from that Eden-like place within themselves, a place of wholeness. If, without turning our teenagers back into children, we can transmit through our voice, our physical presence, and our facial expressions a taste of Eden, we will have accomplished a great deal.

EMOTIONAL CHANNELS FOR LEARNING

Learning is often dependent on the kind of emotions educators transmit. I became aware very early on that my intellectual development was affected by the emotional quality that teachers projected. While sitting in the classroom of teachers who radiated some form of parental affection and interest, I was able to absorb even the most difficult material and earn high grades, while the lessons of teachers who were excellent technicians but emotionally cold simply did not penetrate my mind. As a rule, relationship is the medium through which knowledge and cognitive skills can flow from one person to another. In the *Kabbalah* this is represented by the notion that the light of wisdom can penetrate human minds only when the path is lit by the light of love. The opposite is also true; sarcasm and cynicism on the part of a teacher can close the mind of a student, making it impossible for her to learn. One of my high school mathematics teachers once asked me to solve a certain problem he had scrawled on the blackboard. "I'm not familiar with that kind of problem," I remember telling him. In a tone drenched in sarcasm, the teacher "introduced" me to the problem, "Chaim, meet problem. Problem meet Chaim." The mocking tone of his voice snapped my mind shut. It took me six months until I was able to begin to absorb mathematics again.

The relationship between learning and emotions is doubly important when one is dealing with youngsters from uprooted families or families who have been locked into a cycle of social and economic failure. Almost invariably, children from such families who have succeeded in breaking through to a new feeling of competence and confidence have had the benefit of a teacher with whom they felt an emotional, quasi-parental connection. We must never tire of declaring that children's perception, whether conscious or subconscious, of lack of faith in their ability to succeed may very well be the primary cause of poor academic performance among deprived groups.

Emotions, then, are the key with which the process of learning can be unlocked. One of my mentors, Professor Reuven Feuerstein, is an educational innovator renowned in Israel and internationally. The main thrust of his work has been to demonstrate the possibility of coaxing out the hidden cognitive abilities of children and teenagers labeled retarded or low achievers. One of his educational axioms is that a child who displays a sample of high-level cognitive ability— a single act, for example, of complex reasoning—carries within herself the potential to raise all of her thinking to the same level. But how does Feuerstein elicit this sample? With enormous patience— he may spend hours with a low-functioning child, nourishing her with loving attention, until evoking the evidence of higher ability that he seeks; this moment can be a turning point in that child's life.

Sometimes, unlocking the intellect means building on experiences that the child already knows and trusts. In the case of Tedesse, the young Ethiopian shepherd boy, we asked ourselves how his experience as a shepherd could help him to learn the abstract concepts that are of such importance in the Western educational system. The challenge was to go deeper than merely asking him how many sheep would remain in his flock should hyenas stalk and kill three of them. Could his math teacher get him to talk about the many shades of green he remembered in the meadow, or whether the air smelled different when a rainstorm was moving in? To let him describe the whole two weeks he spent alone, or with another friend or two, circling with the sheep through the hills and pastures. Even though these memories might seem to have little to do with mathematics, they may have everything to do with the process of learning mathematics, with unclogging the emotional channels through which even mathematics must be absorbed. By bringing memories associated with happiness and competence into the mathematics classroom, as well as by creating an emotional bridge into childhood, the subject matter itself will lose its frightening, alien quality. Tedesse indeed showed a new openness to mathematics once his teacher had internalized the link between emotions and abstract learning.

SARAH: *THE GRAMMAR OF NURSING*

Sarah was another Ethiopian teen whose experience at Yemin Orde demonstrates the extent to which a child or teen needs an emotional openness or connection to learn. Sarah came to our village with enormous learning gaps in all the basic school subjects. She was the oldest child in a family of eight and had helped her now divorced mother to raise the other children as she eked out a meager livelihood. Sarah had little psychic energy left over for mastering school. At Yemin Orde she struggled with all of her school subjects, until she had a stroke of luck. Her grammar teacher, Miri, a young woman who had recently married, became pregnant and had a baby. Hebrew grammar is probably the most difficult subject for new immigrant children, and Sarah had shown no particular talent for it, but when she heard that her teacher was home on childbirth leave, she insisted on going to see her. The one thing Sarah knew how to do was to hold infants, and bring them to their mother's breast for nursing. Miri, on the other hand, was completely inexperienced with infants. Sarah showed Miri how to hold her child confidently and naturally, and taught her that her child would not fall apart in her arms. Sarah visited often during her teacher's pregnancy leave, helping her with the initial stages of caring for her baby even as she had helped her own mother.

Then something unexpected happened. When Miri returned to teach, Sarah caught on to Hebrew grammar as if she were a baby learning her mother tongue. Mastering grammar became the key for Sarah to absorbing other subjects as well. Sarah went on to university, where she ended up majoring in linguistics and beginning a successful career as an academic.

Creating emotional channels through which intellectual content can flow is of utmost importance in teaching. It is as if some aura or whiff of parenthood must accompany successful teaching, and all the more so in situations in which parenthood itself has weakened.

8

ANCHORS IN THE PAST

GIDEON

ideon remembered his father Prosper, a police officer, as a man whose bearing and manners expressed the epitome of self-confidence and who was loved and admired by the community he served. He was everything a child might dream of in a father; a hero in the street and a warm and loving parent and husband at home. Despite all the pressures and emergencies that went with his job, Gideon recalls how his father always seemed to be there at bedtime, to tell stories and tuck him in. "How did he manage to be there for us?" Gideon, who now has his own children and a busy career, sometimes marvels.

Gideon's idyllic childhood didn't last forever. Gradually, his father's behavior changed, and so did his personality. Rumors that Officer Prosper was on the take had begun to spread in the community. He began to withdraw emotionally, and his mood swung from brooding melancholy to angry outbursts. By the time the reports reached the local newspaper, Prosper could no longer bear the shame. He was found in a nearby orchard, a self-inflicted bullet wound in his head.

After his death, the family broke apart. Gideon, age 13, was sent to our Village. The crisis his family had endured and the shock of the abrupt loss of the home he had grown up in was evident in his appearance, but so was the strength and stamina he radiated. His anger towards his father was at the center of his emotional vocabulary during his sessions with therapists and counselors. Yet hanging over his bed, concealed behind a larger photo of a giraffe on the African Savannah that could be flipped up, was a passport photo of his father in uniform.

In a recent deep into-the-night conversation I had with Gideon, he talked about some of the insights he had gained into the process he went through after losing his own father. "In a sense my father abandoned me, too," Gideon said, "but somehow I was able to keep him alive with me, despite my anger."

"I remember," he remarked, "the stories you made me tell in the dining hall during Saturday dinners—the same ones that my father told me. When I ran out of good stories from my father, I used to go to the library, read storybooks, and tell them to the others as if he had told me those stories as well. And then, when I was fifteen, I recall stepping out of your office after one of those conversations with a clear direction. The day will come, I told myself, when I will sit at my father's desk, in a uniform just like the one he wore in the photo I had hung, and the community which had humiliated him would know: 'This is Prosper's son.'"

This dream was the glue that helped him rebuild his life. The bright past living on through the stories he had heard in childhood, and the aspiration, rooted in this past, to do honor to his father's name, formed a pathway through the turbulent and agonizing present that allowed Gideon to unify his memories of the past with his goal for the future. The village worked consistently with him in order to make this occur, and there were ups and downs on the way. Yet once Gideon graduated from high school and maneuvered his way into the army as a cadet in the military police, rising quickly in the ranks with much encouragement from us, we knew that his father's desk was within his reach.

TIME AS AN UNINTERRUPTED FLOW

This sort of story is not uncommon in the Yemin Orde Youth Village—a childhood suddenly interrupted by events and forces that children cannot fully comprehend and that are beyond their control, which breaks the normal trajectory of their lives and throws them into new and terrifying circumstances. Our aim in Gideon's case was to ensure that the tragic events and injuries inflicted on his young life would not create an irreparable fissure in his inner experience of the flow of time. This would have damaged his chances to create a unified identity in which the present draws coping energies from the past as well as from a vision, even a vague one, of the future.

A defined and unified identity provides us with the inner strength to continue our journey into the unknown and yet remain ourselves. Endurance in time is perhaps the most basic raw material from which identity is formed. The notion of identity is anchored in the feeling that, despite my changing circumstances, something essential about me remains the same. Without memory, the past that lives on in the present, we would lose our sense of identity, as amnesiacs do. We would forget who we are. If we experience time flowing from past to the future in a broad, uninterrupted stream, it means that our identity is stable. This stability gives us the confidence to believe in ourselves, to explore life and to run the gauntlet of its challenges. This model of identity, one that rests on solid ground yet is continuously graced with a dynamic element, is the kind of identity to which teenagers ultimately aspire.

But for the adolescent just emerging from childhood, achieving this kind of unified identity is a lengthy and painful process, and one that can seem, from his perspective, hopeless. In the training sessions for our new youth counselors we compare the adolescent psyche to a *tel*, a biblical Hebrew term that describes a hill where successive civilizations have built cities, and the archeological ruins of each layer in time jut jaggedly into the previous layer. On the top of the Tel there may be a thin layer of earth, adorned by tall grass and lush flowers in the springtime. But beneath the grass and the flowers are the stones of collapsed houses, scraps of pottery and fragments of assorted tools, whose origins must be sorted out by archeologists whose training and knowledge of historical artifacts prepares them for the painstaking work of assembling these puzzles.

It is hard, especially when confronting enraging behaviors, to re-member that although adolescents may put on a good show of self-confidence, beneath the surface of their psyches are the jumbled ex-periences of childhood that have not yet been assembled within the context of a stable identity. The basic experience of subjective time as an uninterrupted flow is ruptured by emotions that the adolescent may not have the vessels to contain, by memories he or she cannot integrate, or by a numbness that stems from withdrawal from the task of comprehending a painful and complicated world. Experience has taught us that only an adult who has cultivated an inner conviction that the fragments do indeed all fit together, that what we are look-ing at are pieces of a puzzle and not a random heap of debris, will be able to significantly help in the work of integration. If we can keep in mind both the child and the adult, both the past and the future, when looking at our adolescents, we can help create within them an inner space where the fragments can be assembled into a unified personality.

THE UNFINISHED BUSINESS OF CHILDHOOD

At the onset of adolescence, the pain of the bruises acquired in childhood rises to the surface, flooding consciousness with its power. Adolescence, as I have said, is a kind of rebirth or re-creation. Just as in the biblical account of the process of creation "The earth was chaotic and unformed, and darkness covered the surface of the deep," so, too, in the re-creation that is adolescence. Rebirth springs out of darkness and chaos and rubble from the un-chartered depths.

Even a so-called "normal" childhood is filled with trauma. Parents quarrel and show it in one way or another, and no matter how hard we try to hide the harshness that sometimes shadows the most loving relationships, children always know. All couples pass through problems at work, emotional disappointments, the illness and death of relatives and parents. Children absorb it all. Who utterly escapes the pain and sadness that sometimes overwhelm all else in the real world? Children feel whatever is going on in the adult universe, whether inside the family or outside on the street. Although children seem to live in a world of their own, it is a world that needs protection, love and attention from the parallel universe of the adults. When clouds block the sun in the world of adults, the children's universe is also darkened. This darkness can stunt a child's emotional growth, and thus leave indelible marks on their soul.

There is the potential for much suffering within the world of the children as well. Siblings compete for attention and love, hurting each other in the process. Classmates insult, manipulate and reject each other during the course of the years in elementary school. Children are singled out for ridicule—because they are too fat, too short, or have a learning disability. Some suffer physical abuse at the hands of their schoolmates or neighborhood toughs. Even some of the bullies suffer from the shame and guilt of knowing they have caused pain.

Then there are the "little" wounds. A two-year old falls and bruises his knee, and no one is there to hug him and to explain to him that the world will soon be right. A four-year old is lost in a department store for twenty minutes and feels, suddenly, the terror of abandonment. There is the everyday suffering that comes from living in a world not designed for children. Children are often forced to adjust to the urgencies of the adult world as they are dragged from bed, hurriedly dressed and fed, and rushed to school so parents can get to work. In the past few decades children have been confined, in many places, to smaller and smaller spaces, and prevented from wandering freely through our neighborhoods, as many of us did as children, because the streets have become too dangerous and unpredictable. One wound opens another.

Why do the painful parts of childhood become reactivated at adolescence? One way to look at it is that people are instinctually led to at least try to resolve the basic issues of one stage in life before moving on to the next stage. All unfinished business must achieve some kind of closure. Their "Tel" must be excavated. Everything that went on in childhood is part of the material from which teens must forge an identity—and identity, defining who I am, to myself and to others, is perhaps the central issue of adolescence. Nothing that is pertinent to that question can be swept under the rug for long.

The question of identity is closely linked to the question of self-confidence. The child is father to the man because the child has the power to give the gift of self-confidence or to withhold it. That gift is worth its weight in gold to the adolescent. Struggling to leave childhood, the teenager sorely feels the points where his confidence has been weakened because he desperately needs that confidence in order to embark on the journey to adulthood.

THE HEALING POWER OF ADOLESCENCE

The reactivation of the unfinished business of childhood is not necessarily a bad thing. Instead, we can view adolescence as an hour of grace, an opportunity and a blessing, because adolescents possess an abundant store of resilience. The mysterious energy that powers the enormous transformations that characterize adolescence also contains healing powers.

One of the remarkable aspects of life in our village is that there are so many opportunities to witness these powers of resilience and healing. The traumas that are common to many of our village's children often do not have their first cause within the small circle of family. Frequently, it is the cruel nature of the world we are living in that has disrupted the life of the family, forced the children into seeking refuge outside their home, and stripped away the social environment from which the family drew its identity, causing deaths, exiles, and separation. For children who have experienced such losses and traumas, reality sometimes feels like a walk through two distorting mirrors that are facing and reflecting each other—creating a maze of confusing emotions and images. A child may feel doubly cursed, once by the hurt and loss normal to childhood and internal family dynamics, and again by being from a foreign culture or a marginal social class.

LILY: *PLAN VERSUS PLAN*

Lily arrived in Israel after a nightmarish journey that lasted far longer than she ever thought it would. Even then, her hardships were not over; when she descended from the plane, she expected her distant relatives to meet her at the airport and take her to their home. A journalist found her hours later sitting on her luggage and weeping. We learned about her from the weekend edition of the paper, and offered to bring her to Yemin Orde. For us, Lily's story has become synonymous with the way in which parental absence can create not only a vacuum, but a cavity filled with the pus of concentrated human evil. Lily's story begins in a Muslim Middle Eastern country, with parents who were never well-suited for each other, not least because her father was many decades older than her mother.

Lily's mother escaped from her mismatched marriage, threw away the veil she had been required to wear over her face, and reached Europe where she started over again with a new man her own age. Lily's father also left home and disappeared into the mountains. At the age of 14, Lily, disguised as an Islamic nomad from one of the indigenous tribes in the area, made her way to the Turkish border. When she crossed over the border at night, she thought her troubles were finally over, but she was wrong. With no passport or identifying documentation Lily was cast immediately into prison, and in the feminine version of "Midnight Express," was horrendously abused first by the police patrol who arrested her and again later by prison guards.

Lily's resourcefulness in jail eventually paid off. She managed to make contact with the Israeli consul in Istanbul, and remembering the exact names and addresses of her relatives in Israel, convinced him to work for her release. From then on, her path to the airport was clear.

When Lily arrived in our Village, she was emotionally devastated. Her emotional deficits and lack of an inner sense of security and trust in humankind stretched back to her early childhood. The only thing she had going for her, it seemed, was survival instincts and a strong desire to live. This is what had brought her to Israel. Lily was a loner, by dint of the circumstances of her life, and her absorption into the life of the Village through friendships with other children was not easy. As with every child opening a new chapter in their life after trauma, disappointment and wandering, the first stage may seem to involve little more than enjoying the security of food and shelter. Yet we have seen over and over again how crucial this period is in the long term. In Lily's case, as in other cases, all her finely honed survival instincts were attuned to the task of reflecting on the nature of the place in which she had arrived, and puzzling out her conclusions.

Almost as a form of conscious experimentation, Lily produced a battery of "tests" to see how we would respond: sarcastic remarks, curses and vulgar language, direct disobedience of our rules, violence and disappearances. Sometimes I wondered how teens such as Lily are able to create such a sophisticated plan to challenge and explore the crucial question: Who is the adult who is standing in front of me, claiming the role of guidance in my life? This is where the concept of "plan" versus "plan" effectively comes into play. Lily began to settle down as she subliminally sensed that we also had a plan. Our plan was not a syllabus, nor a curriculum, nor a book of rules, nor a list of skills she had to acquire. Instead, our plan was an inner outline meant to form a positive mirror image naturally corresponding to the chaotic "plan" that her bitter experiences had produced. In her acting out, Lily was showing us that the wounds she had suffered had created within her a fragmented consciousness where the past was cordoned off by boundaries of pain, the future obscured in clouds of fear, and her connection to others blocked by layers of mistrust.

Our work was to show her that we saw her as a whole person, with a past that could be salvaged as meaningful even with its pain, a future that we had faith in, and potential we would help cultivate. The vibrancy of life in the Yemin Orde Village where she now found herself, in a completely natural way, began to wear down her harsh reactions to human contact. The lines and circles conveyed by the contents of all our encounters with Lily first manifested in soft pastel colors in the background, and gradually began to emerge sharp and luminous. As Lily began to detect the contours of our "plan"—past, future, earth, sky, and the circles of tikkun—she began to feel more rooted in the existential present and the furious pendulum swings of her behavior began to calm. It took three years until Lily's core of purity and basic human goodness recharged to the point where it could serve as the center of gravity of her emerging adult identity. Years later, when I occasionally meet Lily and others who arrived in our village in similarly devastated conditions, they often ask me, "How were you able to stand me?" What I feel they are really saying, with an almost indiscernible wink, is "You passed my test. Cheers!"

A SENSATION OF INNER TIME

As Gideon's and Lily's stories show, when we create the right conditions, the powers of healing that the adolescent psyche possesses in abundance can do their work. We need to help teenagers feel time as an uninterrupted flow, and feel the connection between their past, present and future. And we can do this by causing our teenagers to feel the past come to life in the present.

Without prying or insisting, and without taking on ourselves the role of psychotherapists, we have to send the message to our teens that they can talk about their open wounds—the gaping holes, pain and uncertainty whose origin reaches into their childhood. Although we keep reminding ourselves that the bridge to children is not through words but rather through our own inner transformation in relation to them, the power of speech in this aspect of the work of healing cannot be denied. Through language, past events can be brought to life and consciousness. We have to encourage and legitimate the verbalization of past experiences. By creating an atmosphere in which aspects of the past can be legitimately remembered and discussed, we conjure within the child a sensation of inner time, time that includes memory and is not confined and delineated by the stimuli of the moment. The child senses the depth-dimension within the vessel of consciousness where healing can take place and from which, as in the case of Gideon, he or she can move forward.

The kind of discourse that has enabled the adolescents in the Yemin Orde Youth Village throughout the years to verbalize pain from the past does not need to take place only in focused and self-conscious bursts of attention, as in therapy. Instead, we try to touch upon the past on many different occasions, as part of a continuing conversation with each adolescent. One way to demonstrate the legitimacy of reflecting on childhood is by referring to one's own childhood. Talking about the pain as well as the joy that you experienced in childhood will create a reality in which articulating memory is acceptable and even encouraged. The challenge, for both teachers and parents, is to create intimacy and reveal personal pain rooted in the past without negatively affecting one's moral or emotional authority. This always takes a certain degree of good judgment. We have to be able to offer personal revelations to our teenagers that will signal the legitimacy of touching childhood pain. But we need to carefully select and express these revelations using the healthy part of our psyche. Ideally, our adolescents need to see us leading the way in exploring complicated feelings from the past, but they don't need to necessarily see us in pain right now. It might be wise to choose to reveal childhood vulnerabilities that have already been resolved, not those that are still gaping wounds.

If we open the path for our teenagers we will see—almost magically, gently and slowly, right before our eyes—the broken shards of the "Tel" gathered up. This is not just a utopian vision. An inner time flow is created. Incidents from long ago are seen as alive and available for reshaping through external dialogue and internal reflection and the parts of experience that were cut off, kept isolated and apart, are magnetized. Pieces come together. Gaps are overcome. A sense of the unity of the personality overcomes feelings of detachment and incoherence.

MAKING THE PAST ALIVE IN THE PRESENT

The past can become present in public as well as private conversations. In A.S. Neill's experimental school Summerhill, children's assemblies were an important component of their community. Imitating in a way the historical Greek Polis, where democracy was born, the focus was on airing and finally voting on regulations, issues and disputes relevant to the day-to-day life in the school. In Yemin Orde, our regular assemblies and group discussions always try to touch on some aspect of our teenagers' pasts, creating an atmosphere in which the past is neither ignored nor denied. Sometimes discussions of current events in the collective life of the village spur children to express traumas from the past, while others listen attentively. Recently, the highway-and-road administration authorities constructed new signs on the highway and road leading upwards to the Yemin Orde Village. Strangely, these new signs, while they indicated the direction to other nearby villages, simply ignored our existence. The youngsters found the old signs thrown into a ditch on the side of the road. The discussion that week was heated. "How dare they wipe us from the map of Israel?" some of them shouted. Although I did feel angry with the authorities, and could think of no logical explanation for why they had done this, I was grateful for this wonderful therapeutic gift. The feeling that our village had suddenly become an abused underdog, ignored and insulted by forces stronger than us, evoked and legitimated wellsprings of concealed pieces of the children's narrative that might have taken hundreds of hours of therapy to emerge.

Individually, I make a practice of keeping doors to the past open by asking each of the youth about their family, hometown, and the school they attended before reaching us. I might ask a youngster about memories from his or her country of origin—about spring in an Ethiopian village or children's songs in Russian. Once, in northern India, talking to children of the Tibetan Children's Village who had left their ancestral homeland behind, I made a point of asking the children what they missed most about home. "Yak meat, the way our mothers know how to prepare it," was the common answer. The Tibetan officials later told me that they did not approve of the question I had asked. "What use is it to awaken feelings of nostalgia and longing among the children?" they said, "We can't get yak meat down here in India. We can't give them home cooked food." I disagreed. "You must let the children articulate their longing," I told them, "or it will gnaw at them from within."

Even feelings of failure can be reinterpreted through dialogue. I'll never forget a young woman named Adina who had no father, a mother who was barely functional, and a grandfather who was constantly in some form of legal or financial trouble. From which parental figure was Adina to draw strength in shaping her identity? It seemed to me that her grandfather was the best bet. I encouraged Adina to talk about him, by asking about him each time we met, and made sure that I was not judgmental in my reactions. Gradually, Adina allowed herself to shape a new interpretation of her grandfather's adventures. She began to see her grandfather as a "rascal" rather than a criminal, which we had no proof that he really was. She now included in her view of her grandfather the idea that he was someone who had an irrepressible love of life, echoing her own verve, that kept getting him into trouble but also allowed him to bounce back again. This reinterpretation of her grandfather's behavior allowed her to release her own powers of resilience and love of life. She was no longer as embarrassed by her grandfather. She could claim him as her own, not as an ideal model for life, but as a precursor passing along a fundamental vitality and passion that Adina could channel in her own directions.

This achievement was not only the result of an isolated series of verbal interactions, but part of a context in which dwelling on the past is normal. We can reinforce this sense of shared fate in many different ways. We can bring our own parents more actively into the lives of our children. We can hang up photographs of ancestors on the walls of our living rooms. Again, we do not need to be aggressive in examining the past. We are not trying to do psychotherapy. We are trying to make the past alive in the present, and thus susceptible to interpretation; to the gentle light of the mind; to the healing powers the teenager himself possesses.

CASTING ANCHORS IN THE PAST

At times, it is desperately painful to attempt to live up to the golden rules you have set for yourself in educating adolescents. We at Yemin Orde have always maintained that an adolescent's awareness and identification with his or her ancestral past is a crucial component in constructing their emerging identity. This principle is for us unequivocally clear and in normal circumstances it is not difficult to provide the connections and content that will enhance and strengthen this fundamental awareness. Yet its determinate importance in a youngster's life means that even in circumstances that are difficult, we have to go the extra mile in order to provide our teenagers with essential links to their collective past. The very effort to find value in the story that is available, even when one has to engage potentially toxic narratives, can itself be perceived by adolescents as an affirmation of their identity.

DESTA

When a highly respected Ethiopian elder was accused of molesting a very young Ethiopian girl, his grandson at Yemin Orde experienced the accusation as a mortal attack on his own honor and integrity, and perhaps even on his very right to live. At a funeral for a family member, which I attended with him, Desta told me, "The next grave will be mine," implying that his grandfather's arrest was evoking in him suicidal thoughts. I hugged him and promised him that he was not alone in this, while asking myself, "How on earth will I be able to show that my promise extends beyond verbal sympathy?"

The newspapers' coverage of the arrest and prospective trial—complete with an illustration of a young girl fearfully gripping a teddy bear and over-shadowed by an elderly man—made me feel even more despairing. I was certain that the police authorities would not have pursued this case without solid evidence.

The weekend editions of the tabloid papers expanded on the story and began to implicate the entire Ethiopian culture as the background for these lurid events. They claimed that a kind of duplicity existed within Ethiopian culture that tolerated sexual crimes under the protective aura of respectability. The newspapers meant to demythologize the Ethiopians, who until now had largely been seen as throwbacks to biblical times in their innocence and purity. As if this case had released a genie from its bottle, prejudices and fears about the exotic other that until now had been repressed began to emerge.

For thousands of Ethiopian Jews, who for centuries had seen their elders as the ultimate embodiment of their culture's wisdom and values, the media reports induced a state of hurt and numbness. The result for the Ethiopian youngsters in our village was a kind of confusion that diminished their ability to function and do their schoolwork. This reaffirmed for me the power of ancestors, as represented by the elderly, to have a tangible and immediate impact on teenage lives, for good or bad.

But for Desta, the issue was one of life and death. We decided that we had to show Desta and the other Ethiopians in our Village that we really stood with them, and with their culture. We decided to form a fund that would combat the negative publicity in the media that was in the process of creating a noxious association between Ethiopian culture and sexual misbehavior. This dovetailed with another principal we hold dear, namely that education worth its name must attempt to shape the public discourse. This existential quality, more than anything else, is what transforms an institution from simply being a warehouse for children—which in the best case provides maintenance and processing—into a true educational entity.

The lawyers, whose hiring was sponsored by Yemin Orde staff members, demanded that experts in Ethiopian culture be allowed to testify as witnesses for the defendant, in order to un-ravel what exactly did happen between the elderly man and the young girl. In that way, we wished to legitimate Ethiopian cul-ture as a crucial nexus from which understanding and judgment about the truth of events could emerge, thus placing it on par with Western observation and judgment. Our law team vigor-ously protested prejudicial statements by the Tel Aviv District Court judge implying that Ethiopian society was primitive, as well as the judge's allusions that sexual abuse was rampant with-in the culture. By enlisting our village and members of the larger Ethiopian community in a battle for the honor of their heritage, we let our Ethiopian children know that they were not alone and at the same time helped them activate their own powers of resistance to the dismantling of their pride in the past.

The lawyers hired by Yemin Orde took the case to the Is-raeli Supreme Court, arguing that the District Court had been stained by prejudice. In several important newspapers the focus of the coverage of the trial changed, as journalists started ques-tioning the stereotypes that the court had disseminated. Every-one in the Village was kept informed and involved throughout the course of the trial, until the day came when Desta's grand-father was released from jail. Although we could not reverse the court's decision, we did manage to secure him an early release. For the community, the message of believing in his innocence and our willingness to fight for it came across strongly.

Desta, I am happy to report, received rabbinic ordination and a degree in education. Married and the father of four chil-dren, he is now a highly respected teacher at the Yemin Orde high school.

WHOLENESS IS HIDDEN WITHIN THE FRAGMENTARY

Our intention was not to clear the elder of charges that may or may not have been true, but rather to ensure that the justice system and media not be allowed to pronounce a verdict on all of Ethiopian culture, and thus rob the younger generation of a major component of their identity. The idea that every young person has the right to be meaningfully connected to her ancestry commits us to sometimes going very far in sending the message that the brokenness and confusion of the present does not corrode our ability to see wholeness and value embedded in the past.

By believing in the value of the past, we become agents of the idea that the potential for wholeness lies hidden within the fragmentary, and can be reconstituted through the active mediation of human will and effort. To set anchors in the past, sometimes it is just as important to engage in a process of facing and clarifying even the darker corners associated with one's older generation. As we do this, we sometimes have the opportunity to widen the circle, to understand the broader context from which our ancestors emerge and to know that no Pandora's boxes remain whose contents we have ignored.

LIVING WATERS FROM THE WELLSPRINGS OF OUR IDENTITY

Through the years, we have learned how the sense of time as an uninterrupted flow, which is essential for the formation of a healthy personality, must stretch beyond personal time. The collective past of the group into which a child is born is as inherently significant to a child as his or her own personal history. What our teenager is trying to forge is not only an inner identity, but also a social identity. A major part of an adolescent's aim is to locate his or herself within the social milieu, both in the boundaries of his or her peer group and within the culture as a whole. They intuit, as well, that success in the future is dependent on their social identity. Although it would be a better world if everyone, no matter which family or ethnic group they were born into, had the same opportunities and the same challenges, teenagers know that this is not the case. Within a child's psyche, the culture and history into which he or she was born can be as significant as their personal experiences during childhood. Teenagers should feel empowered to explore and interpret the meaning of their cultural background, so that it is freed of negative and confining stereotypes.

The amazing capacity children and teenagers have to see themselves as part of something larger than themselves, and to use this larger identity as material with which to build their life, again and again surprises us. We have been privileged to witness this process many times in the context of the Jewish return to Zion from their various far-flung corners of the Diaspora. Over the past twenty years, the mass immigration to Israel has brought hundreds of thousands of Jews from the former Soviet Union, where Communist authorities systematically erased Jewish identity. Hundreds of teenagers from the former Soviet Union have made their way to our Village during this period. Some of their stories provide extraordinary examples of the way in which a teenager can use fragments of information from an ancestor's life to build a new identity.

TANYA: *SLIVERS HINT TOWARD A WHOLE WORLD*

Take the story of Tanya, who grew up as a Provo-Slavic Christian in a small town in the Ukraine. One Sunday, Tanya was sitting with her grandfather in church, and suddenly he leaned over to her and whispered in her ear that he wanted to speak to her outside.

He began, "As a teenager, I was forced into a crowded railway car used for transporting cattle. My family was there, and so were most of the town's Jews. The end of the line was one of the death camps of whose existence we had heard of through persistent rumors. For two days and two nights we rode in the sealed car, the stench of human waste in the stale air becoming nearly unbearable. On the third day I decided that I would try to escape. As the car slowed down I squeezed myself through a crack in the side of the cabin and jumped. Terrified of getting caught, I found my way to a barn and hid. That barn stood right here, on the land where the church now stands. I was convinced that if any of the Ukrainians found me they would immediately turn me in to the authorities. But I was found by a Ukrainian family, and instead of turning me in, they adopted me. A few years later, I married one of their daughters—she is your grandmother."

"Why are you telling me all this?" Tanya asked.

"Because of your voice," her grandfather said, "Now that you've grown up, your voice reminds me so much of my mother's voice that I had to tell you."

Her grandfather's story changed Tanya's life. She read everything she could get her hands on about Israel and Judaism, and eventually brought her grandfather to the Israeli consulate in Kiev, where he proved that he was Jewish by reciting the Shema Yisrael—one of the prayers he remembered from childhood. Tanya's Jewish ancestry was recognized, and she became eligible to immigrate to Israel, where she ended up at Yemin Orde.

If Tanya had heard this story as a young child or as a grown woman, the chances that it would have changed her life in the way that it did would be considerably smaller. But the teenage years are years of transformation, and as such have enormous power to rejuvenate identity. A sliver of a story, as long as that sliver hints at a whole world, can have tremendous potency in the eyes of a teenager.

Hidden Qualities

Another young Ukrainian who found his way to Yemin Orde knew only one thing about his Jewishness. He knew that his grandfather had come from a small town called Uman, "a backwater that nobody has ever heard of" in his grandfather's words. I told this young man that Uman is now the most celebrated town in the Ukraine because it is the place where Rebbe Nachman of Breslov, one of the deepest and most beloved of Hasidic masters, chose to live during the last years of his life, and to be buried upon his death. When talking to Yemin Orde youth I often refer to Reb Nachman's famous sayings and songs, such as "Life is a very narrow bridge and the most important thing is not to fear at all," although I add a stanza, alluding to the youngsters' newly found home, in which the bridge widens and there is no reason to fear at all.

During the years of Soviet rule, the town of Uman was inaccessible. But now, Reb Nachman's gravesite has become the site of a pilgrimage that every year attracts thousands of visitors to the town. "Can you imagine; your great-great grandfather must have been a disciple of Rebbe Nachman?" I have said to this boy on numerous occasions, including when repeating a teaching of Reb Nachman's to the whole school. That one word, "Uman," has become the source from which this young man's entire identity can spring, a source that connects him to Israeli society and to an entire spiritual legacy.

The point is not about Jewish identity, but rather the centrality of the teenage search for identity as a whole. For a number of years now we have been joined in our village every summer by a group of inner-city youth from Baltimore, most of them African Americans. I am always struck by the extent to which their exposure to the ancestry stories told to them by our Ethiopian, Russian and South

American youngsters moves them. They find themselves relating to their own ancestral stories within a new context, free of the discourse of blame and shame that often has otherwise stained their consciousness and influenced their personal development.

Whatever one's family background, there are stories to dig out that are pure gold. A youngster's grandmother might have been a nurse in Jamaica or Tobago. Or their grandfather might have been a fireman in Detroit who risked his life to save a small child. A great-great grandmother may have escaped slavery and earned enough money to free her children as well. Any fragment of a story can be part of an adolescent's life-giving narrative. After years of experience in Yemin Orde we have become convinced that it is indeed possible to reveal in every teenager the hidden desire to find that their ancestors' lives contain a very special hidden quality that represents the secret source of their own strength.

Erasmus is Beating Up Kant

The very physical environment in our village aims to instill a reverence for the past and a feeling of its continued presence in our lives. In one's wildest dreams, who could imagine the Catholic reformist philosopher Erasmus of Rotterdam encountering the staid German philosophical rationalist Immanuel Kant in a fist fight? Yet this was exactly the report I received from a breathless young messenger one unforgettable night, "Erasmus is beating up Kant." What he meant to say in his telegraphic manner was that youngsters from the children's home named after Erasmus were engaged in a row with youngsters from the Kant house. Names like Aristotle, Marcus Aurelius, Sallah A Din, Maimonides, Deborah the Prophet and David Ben Gurion live with the children in their day-to-day life.

Teenagers have the capacity to see themselves as part of something larger and greater, and not only through identification with their ancestors. Their culture and ethnic group, and even the recent history that shaped the reality in which they live, can also be a source of strength, and can cushion and heal the fear of their emergence into a fragmented world. I have often noticed how Ethiopian immigrant children seem less traumatized by divorce than do children from Western families. I believe that this is because Ethiopian culture emphasizes the extended family. Children grow up knowing hundreds of family members going back several generations. The extended family allows broad possibilities for identification and modeling. Surrounded by uncles, aunts and cousins, divorce is far less threatening because it does not touch the extended family, which remains intact as the primary context of family life and a crucible of identity.

ORIGINS ARE FOOD FOR THE FUTURE

A strong sense of identification with one's origins can serve a similar purpose. It can give a child the sense of being held in a much broader embrace, which is steadier and longer lasting than one's individual family and its circumstances. I recall two young teenagers who came to the village after their father murdered their mother—a more terrible or total negation of family can hardly be imagined. These two boys were children of Tunisian immigrants, and I worked hard to reinforce the pride in ethnic origins that was already nascent within them. They graduated Yemin Orde with a strong sense of identification with the Tunisian community that compensated, at least partly, for the destruction of their family. Instead of feeling an utter sense of alienation from their past, they connected to a collective past, placing their private wounds into a broader arena that allowed healing to happen.

Over the years, a continuous involvement in the collective past of all the different groups of adolescents in the Village has become a fundamental part of the Yemin Orde method. There is often a great poignancy to these efforts, because by creating identification and pride, and reinforcing the youngsters' sense of the continuous sweep of time, one is often also touching areas of woundedness and pain.

For example, the Ethiopian immigrants often arrive in Yemin Orde with feelings of cultural inferiority. Ethiopian immigrants come from a technologically undeveloped society into a country where high-tech is associated with high prestige. In Ethiopian villages, cooperative living was the norm; in Israel, the economy currently emphasizes competition, not cooperation. Some of the negative feelings Ethiopian children might have about their culture of origin are based on their own comparisons and inner conclusions. Their parents seem powerless and penniless compared to other Israelis. Israeli society is child-oriented, and immigrant children pick this up by watching television shows or observing their classmates in school and their relationship to their parents. In contrast, Ethiopian culture places great emphasis on the status of elders, and on responsibility to the community. Almost every weekend, children leave their beds and sleep on the floor of the living room in order to accommodate the numerous members of the extended family who often come for visits. But even beyond the children's own resentments and observations, they absorb messages from the society at large. Uneducated Israelis, and even much of the elite, often look at the Ethiopians as coming from "the jungle," from a primitive society less competent, and thus less valuable, than that of the West.

The message we bring these children is that far from being inferior, their culture is, in some important ways, superior to that of the West. We try to show them that the values that guided Ethiopian society contain abundant human wisdom. That the Ethiopian village elders were sophisticated students of human nature from whom our own judges and politicians would be wise to learn. That Ethiopia has a history as long and as varied as that of Europe. Since some sectors in Israeli society—chiefly those ultra-Orthodox who are of Eastern European background—have questioned the Jewishness of Ethiopian immigrants, we bring Ethiopian teenagers an unequivocal message that Ethiopian Jews were one of the most faithful and devout Jewish communities anywhere. We try to imbed these messages in the daily life of our Village. The Village in its entirety celebrates the Sigid, a holiday unique to Ethiopian Jews. The eternal lamp that decorates the village synagogue, residing at its very center, is named for some of the prominent Ethiopian Jewish spiritual leaders. When I first traveled to Ethiopia prior to Operation Solomon, several children a day were dying of disease in the urban slums where the Jewish community lived as they waited to immigrate to Israel. There I met a wise and gentle Ethiopian Jewish elder, Zowdu Zegaye, who was then invited to live full time at the village when the second massive wave of Ethiopian children came pouring into Yemin Orde. Now at seventy, he serves as a living fount of Ethiopian heritage for the children to absorb.

Most of the Ethiopian teenagers are familiar with the parables that adults from Ethiopia traditionally tell their children. We retell these stories, and then discuss their meaning, so that instead of remaining a childhood memory, these parables can become an integral part of their psyche as they reach new stages of intellectual development. They discover, in the process, that the stories their parents told them are far more sophisticated than they once thought.

THE NINTH OF MAY

Yemin Orde makes similar efforts for the children from other cultures as well. That is why every year the entire village celebrates the Ninth of May, the date on which Hitler's forces surrendered to the Soviet army. The Jewish and Israeli calendar year does not lack holidays. Moreover, no one in mainstream Israeli society celebrates May 9th. But on our mountaintop it is a major holiday. The suffering of the Russian people fighting against evil during World War II is a subject that transcends the failures of Communist society, and can be celebrated equally by Jewish and non-Jewish Russians. We try to keep alive the memory of Alexander Sergeyevish Pushkin, the great poet whose birthday we joyously celebrate. And so, in our talks, we inculcate appreciation of great Russian literary heroes, artists and composers whom the teens would have heard about at home but whose accomplishments find little expression in Israeli society. The Russian origin of most of Israel's early pioneers is also emphasized.

In addition, we encourage our teens to keep improving their language of origin. Nothing can replace the deep emotional associations of the language you spoke as a child. Continuing to develop the ability to express oneself in this language gives important access to childhood feelings, and increases the possibility of interpreting them. Thus, our village school offers courses in all the native languages of our students, including Amharic, Russian, and Portuguese. We serve special dinners of Russian, Oriental, Brazilian, and Ethiopian food, accompanied by stories, photos, and films that give a sense of the history and life of the place in question. The message is clear: *Origins are food for nourishing the future.*

9

ANCHORS IN THE FUTURE

The future should be very much on our minds as we reinforce in our adolescents a sense of the past, of where they have been as individuals, as part of a family or a culture. Because when we animate the past, give it vitality for our teenagers within their existential present, we are creating within them a dimension where subjective time can live. Connecting them to widening dimensions of personal and collective history, we deepen their ability to forge an identity that is not lost in the exigencies of the present, but rather anchored in the past and the future, in long-term plans and processes. Don't too many of us feel most alive when we create breaks and ruptures, such as when we abruptly leave a job or a marriage? What we really want our children to feel is that they are most alive through the satisfaction of the continuities they form. We want them to be psychologically fit for the long haul.

When we help our children develop an appreciation for how the past flows into the future like a living stream, we are giving them lungs and legs for running the marathon of life. For along with the courage to experiment and change, our children will need staying power, the ability to make and keep long-term commitments. In love, in professional life, in making a contribution to humanity, the race is not won by the swift, but by those whose stamina is fed by the long view of life, by those for whom the past and future, and not only the present, are real.

The goal is for our children to be able to see the collective of which they are part as an extension of themselves. We are not talking only about legitimizing ethnicity or about creating pride in the minority culture of a teenager's family. Children from the most mainstream of families need to be able to feel connected to their history, to the sweep of time, to locate the thread from which the story of their life begins within the tapestry of history's narrative. Thus it is not enough to merely teach history. Teenagers need to hear that they are part of a history. They need to hear tales of heroism, enterprise or self-sacrifice and to be told that the stories indicate something about their own potential. They need to hear about traditions of wisdom, justice, and creativity, and understand that they are the heirs to these traditions, and that they are the ones who will carry these traditions into the future.

This takes focus on the part of educators. One must see in his mind's eye the way the timeline anchored in the past points right through a teenager's existential present and into the future.

Emotionally as well as intellectually, adolescents need an anchor in the future in order to be able to explore the present, as well as to explore themselves and to experiment with their own identity. The crux of identity is the knowledge that you remain somehow the same through all the transformations and upheavals that the world bestows. Acquiring a stable identity means being able to project your notion of self, your ego, your "I," into the future as well as unifying the fragmented aspects of the past. If I have an anchor in the past and in the future, my "I" will be able to experience the present. But if I have no anchor in the future, I will not be able to be present in the here and now. To the extent that I feel the flow of time as a broad stream passing through me, each moment, each fragment of the present will be crowned for me with an aura of wholeness.

VITTORIO:
SEALING WOUNDS AND TASTING THE PERFECTED FUTURE

Vittorio came to our Village from Milano, Italy. His parents divorced when he was six years old and his mother tried to rebuild her life with a series of men. When Vittorio was 10, his father moved to Israel. Around the same time, his mother became involved with a local man who moved into their household and eventually took Vittorio and his mother to live in a small town in the Toscana region, several hours drive from Florence. Vittorio's mother gave birth to a baby boy, a little brother who came to mean a great deal to Vittorio.

Vittorio had been raised as a traditional Jew and his new stepfather, who was a lapsed Catholic, had in the first flush of romance expressed interest in learning about Judaism and even converting. But when the family moved out of Milan, Vittorio' stepfather returned to Catholicism, and forbade his wife from keeping a kosher kitchen. Vittorio stubbornly refused to give up on his family's religious traditions, which stretched back for centuries. Every week, he would take a train ride several hours long back to Milan, where his paternal grandmother lived. She would cook for him, and provide him with meat for the coming week that she had bought at the kosher butcher.

Vittorio finished elementary and junior high school and began to think about high school. His stepfather tried to convince him that he had better forget about pursuing any career that required academic skill or even perseverance. "You're a nothing, you're a nobody," he would tell him. "You don't have the strength or the concentration to study." Vittorio's stepfather registered him for a high school that taught watch repair, telling him "That's the best you can hope for."

Vittorio was confused. Although his confidence had been damaged by his parents' divorce and his stepfather's hurtful words, he still did not fully accept that his future horizons were as limited as his stepfather portrayed them. The summer before high school Vittorio decided to visit his father in Israel, as if to try to discover another part of himself. His stepfather was livid. "If you go," he said, "Don't bother coming back." "Fine," Vittorio answered. "I won't come back."

When Vittorio arrived in Israel, he faced more disappointment. From what he knew, his father was still single and living alone. But when he knocked on the door of his father's flat in Ashkelon, a city in the south of Israel, he discovered that his father had remarried and had a new infant son. It quickly became apparent that his father and new stepmother did not intend on inviting him to live with them. "The apartment is too small," his father said. But what he really meant was that his new life had no space in it for a teenage son. Vittorio's father offered him a choice of two boarding situations in which he could attend school. Both were located several hours away from Ashkelon—a clear hint at the distance from his life that Vittorio's father wished to keep him. One of them, the one Vittorio chose, was Yemin Orde Youth Village.

When Vittorio arrived in our Village he was withdrawn and surrounded by a cloak of sadness. But within a year, he began to be recognized for the sensitive, intelligent and highly competent person he already showed signs of becoming. In my conversations with him I learned his story, and realized that the open wound of his mother's silent rejection—when his stepfather told him not to come back, she had said nothing, and he did not receive a single letter from her the entire first year he was in the village—needed to be addressed. I encouraged Vittorio to keep writing letters to his mother. "This way, you know that you have acted like a son should," I told him. "One day you will be able to say to her," I promised, "You abandoned me, but I never abandoned you." My subliminal message to Vittorio, which I repeated in various ways over and over again, was: You are stronger than your mother. You are not destined to hurt and disappoint those who love you as she has. I also tried to instill in him the notion that he could draw energies of survival from earlier generations: The degradations of your parents' generation need not reflect on you. Go back further, to your grandparents and beyond. Life takes place along a long axis, it is the expression and realization of all the previous generation —your parents, not you, are the aberration, the weak link in the chain of love and loyalty that has forged your family.

These messages provided Vittorio with foundations anchored in the past and the future upon which he could rebuild his shattered inner world. On the one hand, he had an image of a concrete promise for the future, the day when, strong and confident, he would approach his mother and tell her, "I never abandoned you." On the other hand, he was encouraged in his ability to draw strength from his family's past, as reflected in his grandmother's personality and devotion to him.

By creating anchors for him in the past and the future, we were able to liberate his present, at least relatively, from the threatening grip of past disappointments and his anxiety about the future. Within this island of consciousness, he had space in which to function in day-to-day life and to absorb new knowledge and insights, and to slowly regain his self-confidence.

Vittorio was extremely attentive to the messages that I take care to plant in my open discussions with all the youngsters. Like Fassil, the young Ethiopian soldier who fell under the command of an abusive army officer, Vittorio identified strongly with our oft-repeated saying, "The fox will speak in its own time," meaning, "Be patient. Falsehood eventually fades and the truth will have its day." This sense of destiny and ultimate justice, reinforced by his daily life in the village, helped him internalize the faith that nothing had to be rushed, because that day of reckoning would indeed come.

And it did, sooner than might have been expected. At the end of two years, we supported Vittorio's desire to sample the fruits of future promise by returning to Italy during the summer to visit his mother. With Yemin Orde's help, Vittorio got a summer job washing dishes at a kibbutz. After six weeks, he had managed to save up for a trip to Italy. The rabbi of Florence, who knew Vittorio and his story, offered to drive him up to the village where his mother and her new husband lived. No sooner had they parked in front of Vittorio's mother's home than his stepfather appeared, fierce and grim. "We don't want this boy here," the stepfather said, speaking to the rabbi as if Vittorio did not exist. "It's alright, I just came to say hello," Vittorio said, ignoring the slight. "Your mother does not want to see you," the stepfather replied. The rabbi started the car and began to drive away, but before they had traveled more than a few meters Vittorio saw, through the second story window, a shadowy figure—his little brother. His heart leaped, and he asked the rabbi to stop the car. With a great shout, he addressed his mother, who he still had not seen. "Goodbye, Mama. This is it. You are never going to see me again." Within a few seconds, his mother had raced down the stairs and embraced him.

Their conversation lasted only a few minutes, but Vittorio felt he had won a great victory, as though he had succeeded in planting a flag on the territory of his childhood despite all the attempts to evict him. The effort to allow Vittorio to experience a taste of the perfected future, even before the end of his adolescence, became another turning point on his road to a successful adulthood.

We have seen this process many times with adolescents who have been separated from their childhood homes. If we manage to help them return to the place they left, whether in Eastern Europe, Ethiopia or elsewhere, equipped with new self-confidence and perspective, they often achieve a sense of inner unity, thereby healing wounds previously left open. It is important to know that we don't have to wait until adulthood and its various therapeutic modalities to close the open wounds caused by abandonment. It may not be an exaggeration to compare this process to medical interventions that cure potential defects in embryos before they are born into the light of the world. Adolescents can seal wounds and close circles while still in their teenage years, thus sparing them years of suffering and searching in adulthood.

Nir: *Anticipatory Schemes*

Since childhood, I have had a special craving for chocolate mousse. During the early years of the State of Israel, chocolate mousse was a delicacy available only once a year, on Independence Day. But the best chocolate mousse I ever tasted was only recently, in a small restaurant in south Tel Aviv. The mousse was good, but the taste was sweeter because of the circumstances. The restaurant's owner, Nir, was once a child from a home in which the parents mostly fought with each other. When life at home became unbearable, Nir was placed at Yemin Orde.

Of the many children who have been able to emerge from their childhood chaos, and have actually transformed the materials of their tragic childhood experiences into a life-giving response, Nir's story is almost too perfect an example of poetic justice. Nir hovered over me as I ate, asking me how my mousse tasted every few spoonfuls. Behind him, I could see his father diligently working the cash register and his mother occasionally peeking out from behind a ledge, bringing trays of food out from the kitchen where she was cooking.

"How are they getting along these days?" I asked Nir. "They had better get along," he told me, only half joking. "I told them the first day of work that the moment they begin to fight, they're both fired." I knew he meant it, and by the fact that the work went smoothly, I also knew that they had adjusted accordingly.

I was deeply impressed by Nir's ability to articulate and analyze what had made his parents so violent before and why they were now able to be part of a working team. A crucial part of Nir's rehabilitation at Yemin Orde was our effort to instill in him an anticipatory scheme—an inner awareness of his future possibilities—that his home environment was not able to provide. For all of our children who have emerged from emotionally fragmented childhoods, the ability to internalize that the era of fragmentation is over and that the flow of time is indeed leading to a better place has been continually reinforced by convincing living examples. By exposing the children presently in our care to a constant tide of graduates who had moved beyond their traumatic early years into vibrant young adulthood, we instill in them a clear sense of direction and positive expectations.

Nir, after gaining control of his life, went one step further. He implanted within the fulfilled future a mended form of his broken past, a belated fulfillment of a child's dream. As a child, he was powerless in the face of the bitter arguments that poisoned the atmosphere in his home. Now, with the economic power in his hands, he used it to make certain that his parents would have to work together in harmony.

Including the Future in the Existential Present

To what extent should children and adolescents be encouraged to anticipate adulthood? Medieval paintings often portray children as tiny adults, with sharp, thin faces seemingly already carved and defined by life's travails. In Renaissance paintings, children recover their special beauty, innocence and baby fat. But the nature and meaning of childhood and its relationship to adult life continue to be shaped by historical circumstances and debated by scholars. Are adolescence and childhood time periods whose value and meaning are inherent? Or should these stages be understood and appreciated mainly as a time of preparation for adulthood? This is a question that psychologists and educational philosophers have grappled with at length during the last half century, and, at least in the realm of theory, the child-centered school of thought has emerged victorious. And rightfully so. The "discovery" that childhood is a time that deserves to be treated and considered on its own is one of the great insights of the past generation. For the child-centered educator, childhood and adolescence cease to be seen primarily as an opportunity to shape and influence young lives in order to ready them for the future. This allows parents and educators to let children live in the present, and gives legitimacy to children's own natural paths to self-expression, thus freeing them from the expectation that they be miniature adults.

And yet, especially where adolescents are concerned, the future, like the past, cannot be ignored. Although there has been a great deal of emphasis recently on educating children and teens to be able to function in new and unknown situations, this approach is valid only up to a point. A future that remains entirely unknown, no matter how much training in improvisation is given, will be a source of anxiety for a teenager. The future must also be touched upon, represented, and thus included within the teenager's existential present. If the past and future are not somehow present in the adolescent's here and now, unresolved wounds inflicted by past traumas and the menacing threat looming from an unknown future will shadow their consciousness.

As already pointed out, time is the primary substance from which the mind shapes its identity. The flow of time emerges from *both* the personal and the collective past, and courses toward the future. As much as our psyches are shaped by our experiences in the past, our minds are also structured to anticipate the future. If we perceive the future as threatening and chaotic, we will be too filled with anxiety to live fully in the present.

This is especially true in adolescence. For while children have some capacity to retreat into worlds of their own even when surrounded by evil and cruelty, like the boy in Benigni's film *Life is*

Beautiful, adolescents generally do not have that ability. The remarkable life force that powers their physical, sexual and intellectual spurt toward adulthood is programmed to turn them outwards, towards the real world. When their image of the future in the real world is beyond their grasp, when they have no ability to picture themselves in coming stages of life, teens may attempt to withdraw into a dream world, with disastrous affects. We can imagine the various stages of life as a series of consecutive platforms. But what if the next platform is drifting away beyond our ability to reach it? What if the future is colored not with promise, but rather vague and undifferentiated threat, tinted by the projection of negative past experiences?

Suspended Animation

The future does, indeed, loom threateningly. By the time children reach adolescence, they will have seen thousands of images of apocalyptic violence from the television, movies and comics. They will have absorbed hundreds of sound bites or texts predicting economic, environmental or political disaster. They will have tuned into their parents' anxieties about the future, which has become more complex and less predictable than at other times in human history.

Children and adolescents have a built-in relationship with the future that determines much of their present mode of being and nourishes the contents of their self. Healthy growing up is marked by an increasing ability to infuse rational thought into one's relationship with the future. The "moratorium" from work and responsibility that was created after the spread of industry and the rise of urban centers, was conceived of as a time that would be devoted to preparing youngsters for their role in a newly complex society. Yet what of the emotional vulnerability of young people existing in a state of suspended animation bereft of the status and identity that responsibility and a stable family life proffer?

The teenage years are considered a period during which crucial skills are acquired. Yet they are also emotionally formative. They can be formative in a negative sense if the teenager's relationship with the future becomes so saturated with fear that the idea of the future becomes overwhelmingly burdensome. The teenage years need to be a moratorium, yet one in which self-confidence can grow. It has always been my axiomatic belief that adults have a major role to play in liberating adolescents from the dark, threatening mist that hovers on the horizon for many of them.

THE BOUNCING EFFECT

Moreover, the adolescent concept of the future is vulnerable to what we call "the bouncing effect." Since children's basic feelings about reality are formulated through the prism of their own experience, it is natural for them to "bounce" their experience of the past onto their expectations for the future. A child that has experienced abandonment in the past will most likely fear abandonment in the future. In turn, expectations for the future—which often means fears about the future—are bounced back into the present, in the form of free-floating anxiety. Children stuck between a fragmented past and an unpredictable future will experience a level of fear that does not allow them to abandon themselves to the present.

In contrast, adolescents in whom seeds of faith in the future have been implanted will be better able to throw themselves into the present. This can be seen clearly in intellectual pursuits. Fear and anxiety are one of the most significant obstacles to intellectual achievement, especially in fields that demand problem-solving abilities and the capacity to explore the unknown. Children who lack faith in the future are like Noah's dove before the earth was dry enough to provide her with a perch. She had to keep circling back to the ark—to the same situation, the same patterns of thought.

The poet John Keats once remarked that part of Shakespeare's greatness lay in his "negative capability," his capacity to enter the unknown in his poems and plays without attempting to determine or define their outcome from the start. Shakespeare's characters often meet tragic ends because they lack the very quality of which their creator was so well possessed. Shakespeare's two most famous adolescent characters, Romeo and Juliet, are prime examples. Out of fear that they will be separated they rush to marry, and in doing so neglect to adequately strategize and communicate, or even to fully perceive reality. Romeo, of course, believes Juliet to be dead when she is in fact still alive, and commits suicide himself.

We want our teenagers to develop the "negative capability" that Romeo and Juliet lacked—the ability to be relaxed in the face of what is unknown, and patient before the dark rush of time. Thus many of our arguments with our teenagers have to do with the urgencies they feel, their need to do something "now!" Unfortunately, we often respond with urgencies of our own, instead of demonstrating the patience we want them to learn.

SEEDS OF FAITH IN THE FUTURE

How can we implant in children seeds of faith in the future? How do we create this anchor? The essentially parental quality of good educators means being able to send an unequivocal message to our teens that any kind of abandonment is not in the spectrum of possibilities for them, as far as we are concerned. The fear of abandonment, amplified for many teenagers because of their experiences in their early life and the "unfinished business" of their childhood, is perhaps the primary source of anxiety about the future. We have to instill in our young ones an absolute, unmistakable sense of our commitment to them for as long as we live.

In our Village, the primary way we reassure adolescents about the future is not through words. Teenagers know, both instinctively and through bitter experience, that talk is cheap and promises are made to be broken. On the other hand, concrete lessons are worth a thousand words. We therefore have built a Graduates House, with space for dozens of graduates, in a place in the village that our youngsters pass four or five times a day. Every adolescent at Yemin Orde knows that we consider being part of our community a lifetime commitment—that we never have and never will abandon graduates. They will always be welcome at the Graduates House and in the village.

There are always graduates returning to Yemin Orde, both at high and low points in their lives. Life in Yemin Orde is punctuated by the wedding celebrations we host for graduates, as well as celebrations of their achievements in the National Service and in the academic world. Graduates regularly return to Yemin Orde to teach workshops or organize exhibitions, and give back to the community some of what they have received. Every weekend, graduates join children's tables in the dining hall to tell about their experiences in the outside world and answer questions. Perhaps the greatest gift they bestow is the gift of their presence, which reminds the teens now living in the village that their relationship with Yemin Orde will continue into the indefinite future.

It is not only the graduates who have succeeded, however, who are welcome in Yemin Orde. The Graduates House is meant to serve as a refuge for those of our graduates who are in periods of crisis. This, too, is important for the teenagers who are living here to see. Recently, one of our graduates, Eitan, who had escaped destructive parents and flourished during the latter part of adolescence, was unfortunate enough to experience their toxic influence in his life again. He began a drug and drinking binge that ended in a police lockup in the southern city of Eilat. Yemin Orde sent another of its graduates, one of the first Ethiopian immigrants to study law in Israel, to convince the judge to release Eitan to our custody. Eitan came "home" to Yemin Orde, where he continued to cause havoc, wrecking the room we gave him.

Seeing graduates return to Yemin Orde at times of crisis tells the teens still in our village that our promise to remain in our graduates' lives is unconditional. After Eitan's destructive weekend in Yemin Orde, several youngsters approached me and said, "Now we really understand what you mean when you say you will always be with us."

In looking at our adolescents, it may seem to us as if they are completely absorbed in the moment, and that the future is the last thing on their mind. I have learned over the years, again and again, that in the structure of the adolescent psyche the future is already inescapably present and of real and deep concern. Most adolescents are incapable of or reluctant to express this; in fact there may be an inverse relationship between the willingness of a teenager to talk about the future and the extent to which this concern occupies him or her. Those adolescents who are obsessed with thoughts about their future may be the last ones to share such thoughts. Teenagers may treat their fears and dreams of the future as a sort of pregnancy, where the embryo remains hidden and protected inside its mother's body until it can survive the light of day. Even those children who don't seem to want us to take an active role in helping them imagine the future need us to provide positive reinforcement for their hidden agenda.

There are those who criticize the Yemin Orde method by saying that it fosters dependency. Yet in my experience, only about 10 percent of Yemin Orde graduates need our continued help after finishing high school. Most have gained the self-confidence to make it on their own, and their continued involvement with the village is part of their way to give back to our community. Of graduates that do need our help, only a very small percentage—perhaps one in a hundred—develops what might be termed dependency. Once in a decade, a graduate develops what might be termed *hostile* dependency, something that is hard to bear and is akin to the bad relationships that sometimes develop within families. Yet this is a price we are willing to pay to plant the seeds of confidence in the future in hundreds of other youngsters in our community every year. Like Eitan, this small group of dependent graduates shows the current group of youngsters that Yemin Orde really conforms to the poet Robert Frost's definition of home: "The place where, when you have to go there, they have to let you in."

10

FEELING EARTH

Village traditions are of major importance in molding group coherence and building up individual character and identity. Our annual program includes several long treks through nature, the climax of which is our 106-kilometer long walk from sea to sea—from the Sea of Galilee to the shores of the Mediterranean—which graduating seniors undertake. This year, after the steep and rough climb from the Valley of Jezreel to Mt. Carmel, three of the youngsters sneaked away from where the others rested, made their way to the nearby town of Daliat al Carmel, and returned with several bottles of vodka. During the last part of the hike, which culminates with a village-wide ceremony and celebration—including fireworks and fire-writing—the three arrived completely intoxicated. They pushed their way to the stage, and in front of the stunned audience one of them grabbed the microphone from the MC and began to drunkenly address the crowd. Before the whole village, he lamented that he had no father to appreciate his achievement in finishing the hike. Still reeling in his drunkenness, he also began to expound on the values he had learned in the village—values that he was now, in his view, trampling.

The other youngsters, who had worked equally hard to complete the hike and to produce the festivities, rushed the stage in fury. "What are we, a village of drunkards?" they said. It took a while until things calmed down, but when they did, the village youngsters demanded justice, feeling that their much-anticipated special occasion had been ruined. After a sleepless night, the natural leaders of the seniors decided to take responsibility. "It is not only them, it is us all who should be punished," they said, "We should not have allowed this to happen." They concluded that the most appropriate punishment would be to repeat the cross-country hike again, and to do it this time with dignity until the very end. When offered alternatives to this punishment—we wanted them back in school—they responded with sharp objections. "This is not just. You are lousy educators!" they exclaimed.

The following weekend, to our profound anxiety, the two seniors who had protested most vigorously that the punishment of repeating the hike was the most appropriate one disappeared. They arrived at our gates on Sunday, worn out and covered with dust. They announced that they had backed up their declarations with action, and had just returned from completing again the 106 kilometer hike, thus rescuing their own dignity and that of the entire senior class.

Although this story could be interpreted in a number of ways, the youngsters referred to their repetition of the arduous hike as a self-inflicted punishment. Their concept of punishment reflected what they had imbibed during their years in the village. Punishment emerges from insight and self-choice, is connected to the recovery of integrity and dignity, and includes suffering. Yet it also includes, when you get to the bottom of it, achievement, if not satisfaction.

NOTHING THAT SOUNDS LIKE REBELLION REALLY IS

It is virtually impossible to work with adolescents without at some point dealing with the issues of discipline and punishment. Adolescence is a time of rebellion, although the extent of that rebellion—how long it lasts, how extreme and unyielding it is—will be influenced by the kind of presence a teenager feels in her life from her mentors. Rebellion is natural, but it becomes pathological when it is so powerful that it overwhelms every other aspect of development. Teenagers whose consciousness is colored by the multidimensional presence of a mentor will not need to test reality as intensely and radically as other teens. If educators and parents have managed to open their children to the flow of time and to some form of transcendence, their feelings of being trapped within a narrow consciousness whose constricting shells they must violently crack will be far less pronounced. When parents and educators provide an emotional bridge to the world of adults, teenage rebellion loses its pathological edge.

Part of the adolescent search for identity involves testing the limits and rules that they see as imposed from without; rules that do not have to do with them and their inner feelings and impulses. In fact, children and adolescents do not fully grasp the most basic rule of life, that of causality. They do not yet fully understand the fact that actions have consequences. Rebellion is a way of experimenting with the laws of causality while testing their own strength, and testing the strength of the significant adults in their lives from whom they receive guidance. Adolescents have a sharply developed intuition that allows them to hone in on the weaknesses of both the systems of rules in the home, school, or society they are living in, and the specific weaknesses of their parents, educators, and other adults. That is why teenagers succeed so often in enraging us. But although it often seems as though our teenagers want to destroy our authority, this is not their intention. They want to give us their best blow, and yet see us standing strong. Our ability to respond wisely to their provocative behavior restores their self-confidence in us as models and guides.

We don't usually understand this, at least not during those moments when we are being tested. We tend to see our teenagers' acting out, extreme language and defiant behavior as a personal insult, and as an expression of his or her deepest feelings about us. We feel teenage rebellion as a rejection of the wisdom and values that we are attempting to transmit to the next generation—and thus as a mark of personal failure. Experienced in this way, teenage insolence and defiance becomes a painful and almost intolerable blow to our own self-conception and self-esteem.

It is a mistake to think that the dialogue ignited by the tensions between us is the real dialogue that is going on. This is where the framework of the two lines and two circles can help us. The horizontal line running between past and future helps us remember that the interaction that is taking place right now is part of a far more extended story that began in infancy and will end in adulthood. The vertical line points to the fact that every interaction, especially those that have the potential to explode into verbal or even physical hostility, will be seen by teenagers as a test of our ethics and ideals. Are our ideals strong enough to keep us calm and give us presence of mind even when we are provoked? The circles, perhaps most importantly, call our attention to the depth dimension of our child's psyche, reminding us that what is happening on the surface is only the tip of the iceberg. The two lines and two circles can help us organize our mindset around the insight that nothing that sounds like rebellion really is rebellion.

Although our children have a rich inner life, their emotional vocabulary is limited, their ability to express feelings in words not yet fully developed. Teenagers are generally dualistic in their perceptions; they often see things, including relationships, in black and white. They are manipulative, without necessarily being conscious of their manipulations. However, we should not allow our adolescents to set the psychological and moral tone of our encounters. We cannot afford to regress to the manner or lingo in which a teenager might speak to us. We have to lead them forward. We have to understand that the voice of rebellion is the voice of testing, of trial and error. It is not the adolescent's inner voice. We must never allow ourselves to attribute evil to them. Everything they do, unless they damage or endanger others, should be interpreted as an expression of their feelings, within a vacuum of unconditional acceptance. The teenager's message will be one of separation, "I don't want to see you, I don't want to listen to you, I reject your values and your rules." Our response should be to perceive him or her as part of a circle that includes ourselves. Their message of separation should be met by a message of inclusion. When it is time for me to respond to rules that have been broken, or lines that have been crossed, my commitment should be to the child in question, not to the rules.

On Punishing as an Insider

Even when we have to punish, the message we should give to our teenagers is that their efforts to break away, to test us and their independence, will not cause us to abandon them. Yes, we do have to set limits for our teenagers. They need and want limits. And yes, we do have to correct behavior that harms them or others. At the same time, we have to take care not to use punishment as an opportunity to clip our adolescents' wings. We need to avoid sending the covert message that their efforts to separate and become independent will cause us to cut them off from us.

Matti, an immigrant child, steals from his roommates, from the village offices, even from the museum gift shop on class trips. Obviously, this kind of behavior cannot be tolerated, because it is antisocial at its roots. We need to use punishment as a tool to weaken Matti's desire to steal, otherwise his behavior will continue and will likely escalate, ultimately bringing disaster down upon him. Attending to the problems that Matti expresses through stealing will take much more than punishment. But punishment is necessary also for its public dimension; in order to affirm and underline acceptable and unacceptable norms of behavior.

How should we punish? One of the main lessons our work in the village has taught us is that one must not punish in an emotional vacuum. Punishment must be in the context of a relationship. There are many reasons that teenagers misbehave. We've talked about their desire to test their strength, independence and the significant adults in their life. But there is always an element of pain in negative behavior. This pain stems from hurt and anger over the unresolved wounds of childhood and the confusion and threat emanating from an uncertain future. In order to punish, you first must have a connection to the adolescent's pain—to be his or her partner in dealing with pain.

The way to do this is by connecting to an adolescent's inner feelings, their intimacy. What is it that he or she is ashamed of? What is he or she proud of? What are they hiding? What are they afraid to speak about? He or she may be missing a pet cat that died or that their parents gave away. Or ashamed that they have not yet begun to develop physically the way classmates have. He or she may be proud of their musical ability, or the way they do their hair. The place where an adolescent is wounded, the source of their anger and frustration, and thus misbehavior, is on the inside. Therefore you must punish him or her as an insider, from a place of "tikkun," of insight. You must not punish someone for whom you are not an insider, part of their "intimacy." You don't necessarily have to verbalize the knowledge that makes you an insider. But you do need to connect, in your own consciousness, to your adolescent's inner feelings and struggles. Punishment should not be perceived as coming from a stranger, nor from someone who is making his or herself into a stranger by hardening their heart. A teenager should, first and foremost, see punishment as coming from someone who cares.

How do you establish yourself as an insider? It all rests on your previous connection with the adolescent. It happens when the adolescent is familiar with your own story of failures and successes; is aware of your being a three-dimensional human being who has traversed a similar path to the one he is walking along currently; recognizes you as someone who sets boundaries for him—and yet has in the past had the personal experience of adults setting boundaries for you.

MEANINGFUL PUNISHMENT— DNA (DIALOGUE, NEGOTIATION, AGREEMENT)

Another rule of thumb at Yemin Orde is that there should never be a punishment that does not have an element of choice in it. This means that punishment must always be preceded by dialogue and negotiation. From the adult perspective, dialogue is an opportunity to turn misbehavior and punishment into a trigger for insight. Presenting some kind of choice in punishment allows a teenager to maintain his or her dignity, and to feel that he or she is not simply being bullied by a dictator or victimized by an arbitrary system. Dialogue, negotiation, and choice nourish the part of the teenager that is expressing the inner drive towards independence in pushing beyond the rules. It sends the message that our intent is not to crush this independence, but to nurture its emergence. In whatever way possible, punishment should be meaningful.

In some cases, we need to distance our children from the context in which they have been misbehaving, while also trying to create a situation in which distancing is also a form of healing. In punishing teenagers we need to always keep in mind the fluid nature of their personality, which is still developing. The last thing that we want to do is to create a fixation on the unresolved wounds and fears that led to misbehavior.

It is also vital that we are always conscious of the boundaries that delineate punishment that is healthy and constructive from that which is complicating and destructive. Imposing punishment in an authoritarian way, from above, for example by having the same set punishment for every "crime," or even for every time the same misbehavior repeats itself, may satisfy our desire for consistency and order. It may even work to the extent that it succeeds in eliminating unwanted behavior. Yet shocking a rat in a laboratory achieves the same effect. This kind of punishment is only effective on the outside. On the inside, it is counter-productive, because the scars it creates mark off the pain and confusion that led to the misbehavior as a danger area, thus blocking insight and healing. Instead, by using misbehavior as an opportunity for dialogue and negotiation, for exploring the ethical implications of actions and the emotional charge they carry with them, acting out and subsequent discipline can become a catalyst that moves an adolescent towards maturity.

Moreover, in punishment as in everything else, teenagers see the significant adults in their life as models. Even their rebellion is part of a symbiotic relationship that is based on a very strong inner identification. Punishment provides an opportunity to learn. If teenagers perceive the adults in their life as imposing punishment that is designed to shrink and imprison the spirit, it will contribute to the creation of diseased souls. If punishment and what leads up to it involve creativity and are geared to produce insight and reflection, teenagers will take this example with them into their lives.

The process requires much confidence and faith in the methodology. One needs to be able to sit together with a youngster who breaks rules and takes the liberty to do as he pleases, and have a discussion. This requires a previous connection with the youngster—and a great deal of patience. The process begins with the very quality of time that is dedicated to the inquiry, with the fact that someone is willing to sit and decide together on a healing process, with both sides taking part.

We had a child at Yemin Orde who was known for "bringing the street into the village"—bullying, drinking, and exhibiting all kinds of negative extroverted behavior. Our mission was to turn this behavior on its head, to have him instead "bring the village to the street": offering village values to the outside world. The "correction process" included a hike with his counselor during which long stretches were completed in total silence—as a counterpart to his often loud, provocative behavior. At the end of the process, this young man joined an initiative to pave and otherwise upgrade pathways along the countryside for the disabled.

Never be Ashamed of Shame

We should continuously remind ourselves that the ultimate aim of any punishment is to help create within our children's psyche the capacity for self-reflection and self-critique. This capacity is crucial if our children are to continue to learn and grow all through the course of their lives. They must be able assess what their boundaries are in every given situation, and must eventually learn to think clearly about the consequences of their actions for good and evil. Self-critique is a double-edged sword. The wrong kind of self-critique—harsh, repetitive, and unyielding of insight—can paralyze and stifle energies and passions instead of liberating them.

Self-critique can lead to insight only if it is founded on a deeper layer of emotional openness, an ability to feel and even welcome the purging sting of shame. How often have we cringed at what we perceive as the shamelessness of our young people's behaviors and attitudes? Yet have we ever considered whether we have created a slot for their shame, a legitimate place within their psyche for shame to be expressed? Have we found the space within our discourse to share our own moments of shame when growing up?

In our staff training, we often repeat the idea that if the biblical prophets were alive today, they would compose elegies lamenting the disappearance from the world of the category of shame. If there were shame, there would be less reason for punishment, because shame is the most refined form of self-punishment. Overtly, it seems like shame has been excised from our lexicon of acceptable emotions because it runs counter to the prevailing cultural demand that we accept ourselves, no matter who we are and what we have done. Subliminally, however, isn't it possible that it is the very brittleness of modern identity that has made the notion of shame almost taboo? The experience of shame has become obsolete within the anonymity of urban life that replaced the familiarity of the village and extended family. In front of whom are we to be ashamed when intensive togetherness no longer exists?

One of the contributions of the Ethiopian children to Yemin Orde Youth Village has been their demonstration of the particular role that shame played in their cultural environment. When they detect a reason for shame, they cover their faces with both hands and produce a short sound of embarrassed laughter. Shame is a built-in human emotion; observe very young children encountering strangers and you will see them blush and hide behind their mother's skirt. By repressing it, we block our access to "dangerous" or humiliating memories. Hidden from our conscious minds, these lay embedded with a radioactive toxicity. Under these conditions, in the absence of shame and inner dialogue, paralyzing guilt can emerge to fuel irrational, acting-out behaviors and cause lasting damage to the personality.

In our village, our message is that shame is a legitimate emotion. We want the children to internalize an insight that they should carry with them through life—*one should never be ashamed of shame.* Every year, we repeat the story of the King of the Khazars, who in early medieval times searched for the true religion, eventually engaging in a lengthy discussion of Judaism with a learned rabbi. At some point in their conversation, the Khazar King confronted the rabbi with the incident of the golden calf, a biblical story that places the Jewish people, who the rabbi was defending, in a very bad light. "You have shamed me, King of the Khazars," the rabbi says. Then, emphatically, we drive home the association in the story between royalty and shame: "A person who knows how to be ashamed is himself a king," we say. "To realize that you have committed wrongdoing or have experienced humiliation and yet not to be destroyed by that knowledge, that is greatness!"

By associating the capacity to feel shame with the quality of greatness, shame's potentially corrosive influence on young egos is neutralized. The ability to reflect on painful memories without fear of drowning in humiliation opens the way for learning and growth and paves the way for meaningful inner dialogue. It also does something more: it allows psychic channels to childhood that may otherwise have been sealed to remain open and intact. Teenagers feel that they are what they have the potential to be, but they also know deep inside how small and powerless they are. All those things that cause them to be ashamed are thus repressed. When we teach adolescents to be able to say "I was ashamed, and that's ok," then we have given them the vessels to deal with their weakness.

11

ON HONOR AND TIME

I will never forget Suzy, a startlingly beautiful young woman whose lovely exterior, of which she was well aware, hid a troubled inner world emanating from a tragic childhood. One night in August she failed to return to the village. The next day, as I was on the phone trying to get an update on her disappearance from the police, she appeared at my office door, her body covered only by a skimpy bathing suit and a towel. Behind her stood a bashful, muscular young man, 6'5" tall, as blonde as she was brown. "I found him at the beach," she told me, "I'm going with him forever." Relieved at the very fact that she was alive, I also understood the whole story in a flash—an explosion of hormones!

"You're not going anywhere," I told her, "You're staying right here." "It's my life," she said defiantly.

Meanwhile, outside my office, a group of young men and women had gathered, jealous and fascinated (a number of broken hearts among the men), and all fiercely attentive to the question of where this meeting was going.

Allen, the young man, was from a northern European country. "What do you want from her?" I asked him. His answer came in broken Hebrew but correct grammar, "I really love her." From the tone of his voice and his seriousness, I understood that he had qualities that could not readily be seen as he stood in his wet, sandy bathing suit. My quick decision, to invite him to stay with us in the village, proved to be the right one. Now, fifteen years later, reminiscing about that strange beginning of a wonderful union, Suzy can explicitly attribute her attraction to Allen to the kind of personality he was. He was outside the game of all the hunters who were after her as a conquest for status. During the 24 hours they spent together on the beach, it turns out that they were not indulging in orgiastic sex, but talking about their respective families' stories and his search for his Jewish roots. They now have four children, a warm family life and an ongoing involvement in wider circles of caring and compassion.

The mistake in perception I committed when I initially presumed that Suzy and Allen's sexual attraction was devoid of a larger context is a common one. Most of the books and curriculum on sex education for adolescents concern themselves with specific, quasi-technical questions such as "Under which circumstances should birth control be provided?" and "What we should tell our children about masturbation?" Yet the extent to which teenage sexuality expresses complex social quotients is largely ignored.

Far from being a function of raw animal desire, teenage sexual indulgence and promiscuity is greatly influenced by the search for social status. Often, the linkage between sex and status in the teenager's universe mirrors their understanding of the world of adults. In the absence of a meaningful and multi-dimensional intergenerational dialogue with adults, adolescents will tend to grasp what is called the "social weave" as a well-policed but very shallow web. The "level" a person has reached on the social ladder is defined by his or her sexual partner, sexual visibility, and, in slightly different ways for young women and men, the extent of their sexual experience. When no alternative center of gravity has been created to anchor them in the past, future, earth and sky, adolescents often attempt to procure their identity using the coin of sexual experience.

This tendency is especially acute among teenagers growing up among adults who are not actively involved in creating community, adults who themselves live in a world where romantic and sexual attachments define social status and rank, and in which divorce is prevalent and the family a threatened institution. When adults look and act like teenagers, and lose their status as guides and mentors, then the world of the teenager unites with the world of the adult and the sexual mores of the adult world tend to penetrate into the teenage universe. The opposite is true as well: when a center of gravity that holds both the teenagers and their parents together in a single circle is created, the need to prove one's status through precocious sexual activity and conquest is diminished. Ultimately, the kind of emotional and intellectual dialogue that a young person develops with his or her lover will reflect the quality of the dialogue experienced with the adults in their life.

Much the same dynamic is at work where teenage violence is concerned. Teenage perpetrators of violent acts nearly always describe their motivation as survival, which in their world means the protection of their honor. The desire to live is what creates violence, because honor is survival, the sole and essential quality of their existence. Although to adults it might seem as if the increasingly violent world of teenagers makes no sense at all, for the teenagers, violence is almost always a response to a perceived defilement of honor. Without the framework of the concentric circles and the horizontal and vertical lines, the inner point of honor has no context. When we are involved with past and future, and transcendence, then our honor is not so exposed and sensitive. Bereft of context, the sense of honor becomes an unguided missile. When we succeed in inculcating a sense of gravity and ballast secured by a broad context of emotional connections and intergenerational contacts, there is very rarely violence. This is true as much for schools as it is for individual families. Everyone is able to see things from the other side, to encircle each other, to trade points of view.

IN SEARCH OF LOST TIME

According to Donald Winnicott, a pediatrician who became, after Freud, one of the greatest of modern psychological theorists, mourning for the loss of childhood is a distinguishing characteristic of adolescence. In childhood, time has an infinite quality to it. A twenty minute recess can seem nearly endless, and the three months of a summer vacation feel like eternity. This almost dreamlike quality of time partly explains the capacity of children to become lost in a world of fantasy. But with the onset of adolescence comes a new sense of time, marked by dramatic physical and emotional changes and no longer infinitely expansive. The journey to adulthood has begun.

Those teenagers whose childhoods have been marred by trauma, abuse, or deprivation enter adolescence with a feeling of loss, as if they have been robbed by fate of the paradisiacal time of childhood. Of course, almost every child feels deprived in some sense; those who have siblings, for example, have had to compete for and share their parents' love, while those who don't have siblings feel deprived of siblings. And even for children who have lived exemplary "normal" lives, it is still undoubtedly difficult to adjust emotionally to the new sense of time that has imposed itself on their inner consciousness.

This is perhaps why so many teenagers have difficulty with the strict kind of schedule that the modern world and the modern education system impose on them. And this is why, in our village, we try to be both firm and flexible in terms of time. We are firm in the sense that events—waking up in the morning, prayer services, meals and classes—are all run according to a quite strict schedule. For example, I will never allow teens in the village to see me walk in late for an event. In my estimation, it is often better for me to miss a meeting altogether than to come late. I demand promptness from the rest of the village staff, so that our teens can learn through personal example. We want teens to get used to the idea of exact times, because that is the way that the world they will eventually inhabit works. This is especially important because some of our youngsters, those from the Ethiopian immigrant community and from the Caucasus in the former Soviet Union, have grown up with parents from rural villages who have a completely different, and a much more fluid, conception of time. In pre-modern society sunrise, noon, and sunset, the phases of the moon, and the seasons of the year measure time, not the abstraction of the clock. Part of full absorption into the mainstream of Israeli life is bound-up with becoming familiar with exact notions of time.

While the village and its staff run by the clock, we don't automatically expect the same from every youngster, and certainly not all at once. If children come from a place where discipline was not imposed, or from a place where too much discipline did not allow space to breathe, it is wrong to expect or enforce instantaneous change. At Yemin Orde, we leave room for negotiation and dialogue so that our teenagers don't feel their inner sense of time trampled over by our demands. By allowing flexibility, we offer some kind of compensation for the loss of childhood time. Alongside the abstract time represented by the clock, and without denying its importance, we try to consider inner time as it is experienced within each person. The framework of exact time must exist, both for the functioning of the institution and in order to create structures and boundaries. But by legitimating flexibility, by not insisting that each child follow a rigid schedule with total consistency, by allowing adolescents to flow between their own personal, inner sense of time and the demands of the institution—sometimes emphasizing temporal boundaries and sometimes relaxing them—time can stretch and the loss of childhood can be sweetened.

Let Them Sleep

What is true about class schedules is certainly valid in regards to sleep. Sleep is one of the most personal, inwardly directed activities in which we engage. During sleep, the depth dimension of the psyche finds the time and space to express itself in dreams. The tumultuous psyche of the teenager needs sleep in order to work out the confusing changes he feels within himself. Teenagers also use sleep as compensation, as comfort for pain or loss. One of the lessons I have learned about teenagers over the years is that sometimes you just have to let them sleep. Sleep can be like a cocoon in which a teenager wraps himself, only to emerge much later as a butterfly. Earlier, I mentioned a teenager who came to live at Yemin Orde because his mother was in a mental hospital. We let this young man sleep almost to his heart's content, pretty much constantly for three years. Now he is blossoming. His psychic energies have been renewed, he is ready to face the world, and he is both self-confident and intellectually curious.

Which is not to say that in letting teenagers sleep you don't keep reminding them that they really should get up and participate in life. And sleeping too much can be a warning sign of involvement in drugs—that also needs to be examined. Even when we let children sleep, we do so after waking them, urging them to get up, and making a great show of defending the logic of the schedule. Our message is that the schedule is there, it is important, but we are not going to impose it by coercion. Discipline imposed solely by force will bring with it opposition, conflict and frustration, because it makes impossible demands. You can force things using punishment, by preventing pleasure and through other strategies. But then the basic experience will be of force, without any possibility of insight. This will stunt a teenager's development. We are willing to give a child time until he or she says, "Ok, I am ready." And, if you have faith in them, they eventually will be.

Parents and educators sometimes interpret a teenager's lethargy or desire to sleep as a form of rebellion. This is almost never the case. Once it has been established that their weariness is not drug-induced, we can assume that the teenage need for sleep stems from a lack of psychic energy, which they often feel as lack of physical energy. There is just too much going on within; too many contradictory external and internal demands. The system shuts down, retreats. The teenage appetite for sleep is often what psychologists might call "a regression in the service of the ego." We mentioned earlier that the teenage years are like another birth, another infancy. Teenagers sometimes have a deep desire to crawl back into the womb—under the covers, with the blanket pulled over their heads. Even when it is necessary to push a teenager to get up on time, it is important to remember not to act as if their desire for sleep is a personal insult.

During the moratorium years of adolescence, we have to give a chance, as much as possible, for each teenager to create an order in their life that comes from them and that arises organically from within. This will not happen in a vacuum, simply by letting them alone. We need to present them with a schedule, with the idea of requirements and responsibilities. We need to have a continuous dialogue with them about being on time, about getting up in the morning, about sleep. But we must also avoid causing the scars that come from a relationship organized around the idea that our authority makes us strong, while their youth makes them weak. Teenagers should not get up in the morning simply from the power of threat. Although, as we have said, teenagers are resilient, they are also vulnerable. Defeating a teenager, inflicting negative blows, can cause damage that is difficult to repair. Although we may feel it is our task to make sure that the teenagers whose lives we are helping to guide gain the skills they need for survival and success, sometimes it really is better just to let them sleep.

12

A MIRROR IN THE SKY

When teenage lives are devoid of faith, attempts to find meaning in the face of their apathy and destructiveness are destined to failure. Unfortunately, too often the very mention of faith is immediately associated with organized religion and summarily rejected as a legitimate ingredient in the formation of our youngsters' emerging personalities. Adolescents deserve the word "faith" to be born anew for them, redeemed from the connotations and implications in which it has been imprisoned for so long.

SASHA: *INNER EMOTIONAL LOGIC*

Sasha, a teenager from Russia, taught me a lesson about the possibility of the rehabilitating the word faith. Sasha's exposure to the story of Abraham—who Judaism considers the first adherent of monotheistic faith—was a terrible shock. Of all the stories he was introduced to at our village, the biblical story of the Binding of Isaac, in particular, gave him the chills. "I never want to be part of a people whose founding father was willing to kill his son," he said. Sasha reacted contemptuously, dismissing with a single remark the option of embracing the people of the book and making their story part of his identity. In situations like this we try to remind ourselves to accept every reaction of a young person as a legitimate representation of his current emotional and cognitive state while understanding that further interpretations and responses will come in due time. During the next three years, Sasha had many opportunities to express his reservations or outright rejection of religious beliefs, often emphatically declaring himself an atheist during group discussions, and openly flouting religious conventions and rituals by appearing in synagogue from time to time with his own anti-religious literature. In contrast to his expectations, he wasn't chastised, nor did we attempt to persuade him to change his beliefs. The discussions we held were not geared toward anything resembling religious indoctrination, but instead underlined and flushed to the surface many of the fears and dilemmas he was struggling with in day-to-day life, so that they could be addressed as legitimate and normative. In spite of the transcendent context of the Torah dialogues, he gradually grasped their connection to real, earthy life.

The image of a father with a slaughtering knife at his son's neck is indeed a dreadful one. It is no wonder Sasha that felt that the knife bent over Isaac's neck was also bent over his own. The story of Abraham and Isaac, and Sasha's reaction to it, reveals the nature of adolescent spiritual search, which we rarely are able to recognize. Sasha's world was understandably shattered by the story of human sacrifice. The theme of intergenerational threat dramatically cut through to the chaos at the heart of the adolescent's inner world, arousing memories of threats he accumulated during years of viewing TV and absorbing the narratives of violence so prevalent in contemporary reality and fantasy. Yet Sasha's insistent rejection of the story paradoxically revealed a wish to engage in a search for his identity.

Whenever we are confronted by assertions from our teenagers that seem like capricious rejections of our most cherished values, we need to have faith in our teenager's inner emotional logic, even when it is not as crystal-clear as it was in Sasha's case. These stances represent an attempt to engage in an ongoing, subterranean dialogue with us in which a transition from extreme to extreme may stretch over the course of years. There is an inner dynamic to the provocations that youngsters repeatedly throw in our faces that stems from their search for a separate identity.

Confronting these challenges to our values head-on creates a battleground on which we can never win. Instead, we need to understand the spiral form in which insights are gained. It took Sasha three years to realize that the very story that provoked him so bitterly deserved a different interpretation. Sasha eventually concluded that the story of Abraham and Isaac in its wholeness is a repudiation of human sacrifice in a world in which it was a normative practice. The process that Sasha went through, which began with a convergence between his own raw and exposed emotional state and the harshness of some parts of the biblical story, led eventually toward healing insights that were eventually integrated into his spiritual worldview and personality.

"There are no atheists in foxholes." In some ways, raising a teenager is like being in a foxhole. It is hard to survive the experience intact unless you have faith, and can convey this faith to your child. In Sasha's story, what enabled faith was not religious indoctrination but the opportunity, like Abraham, to experience shattering and despair in the face of an unacceptable reality, human sacrifice, and yet find himself ultimately able to raise the banner of the absolute value of all human life.

The kind of faith we need in order to raise children is not necessarily religious faith in the classic sense. Yet guiding our adolescents into adulthood is a spiritual task of the highest order that necessitates our identifying and drawing on the deep sources of our faith in life. The faith that we find within ourselves can be an opening through which we teach our adolescents about faith—faith in themselves, in life, and in the existence of transcendent values and meaning. In this sense, the transmission of faith is at the heart of the entire process through which an adolescent emerges into a whole adult.

COMFORT BEYOND WORDS IN THE MYSTERY OF LIFE

For many centuries, the connection between education and spirituality was taken for granted. From the time when humans lived in hunter-gatherer tribes until the scientific enlightenment, maturation, in addition to the honing of survival skills, meant the absorption of spiritual knowledge and values. Adolescence was marked by a rite of passage in which each young person would have to demonstrate some kind of mastery of his or her culture's spiritual tradition. For some Native American tribes, for example, this rite was a vision quest; a physical and spiritual ordeal meant to culminate in a revelation. In the Jewish tradition, the "bar mitzvah" celebrant, who has just reached adolescence, is meant to demonstrate familiarity with the Torah and the prayer services and to offer an original interpretation of a religious text. In various forms of Christianity, catechism and confirmation ceremonies mark the period of coming of age.

For the past two hundred years, much of the Western world believed that scientific knowledge could replace religious truth in guiding humanity. Thus, just as adolescence began to emerge as a distinct period in which young people were meant to acquire the skills they need for adult life, Western society, to a great extent, stopped thinking about the spiritual component in education. Now, in the post-modern age, we have painfully come to understand that science is a magnificent tool and an inspiring expression of the human spirit, but it is not going to solve all of humanity's problems. In fact, science's ability to shape and transform the natural and human environment may in fact intensify some of these problems. After decades in which much of educational theory has purposefully ignored the question of spirituality, it is time to renew an ancient discussion whose focus is spiritual education. We cannot continue to rob our children of an essential part of their humanity: the capacity to feel holiness, to touch transcendent meaning.

We do not necessarily need to make our teenagers religious, but we do have to acknowledge the facts of the human condition—that we need some kind of approach or relationship with the transcendent.

TRANSCENDENT PARALYSIS

And yet the transcendent can also be deeply problematic. Conceived in a one-dimensional way, the transcendent can paralyze and terrorize. Religious fundamentalism—whether Jewish, Christian, or Islamic—in its efforts to separate believers from the "impurities" of the surrounding world, can create mental walls that lock our children into rigid and defensive patterns of thought, or cause them to abandon faith altogether. Our job as parents and educators is to try to clear a path for our children toward faith and ideals that heal rather than harm. How can we free religious education from the tendency to lock children into inflexible forms of faith that will either stifle them or that they will eventually reject? What kinds of goals should we set for ourselves in the spiritual education of our teenagers? Although we at Yemin Orde are rooted in a particular religious tradition, that of traditional Judaism, we hope our discussion will be just as relevant for members of other religious groups as well as those whose faith cannot be defined in terms of any organized religion.

Teenagers need an anchor in a transcendent source of value and meaning in order to move with confidence towards the realization of their dreams. The anchors of past and future are necessary because our human identity is inextricably connected to memory and to our capacity to imagine and anticipate the future. But without an anchor in the transcendental, we would have no way to assess our lives, or to put them into perspective. Like sailors in the open sea who depend on the North Star for navigation, only something that rises above them bright and steadfast can provide our teens with the immovable point of reference they need in order to make sense of their journey and their lives.

There is one great difference between the stars and the metaphysical heavens. The stars shine brightly no matter what we think or do. But the "sky" that we are talking about, the top of the vertical line of our framework—the spiritual or transcendental anchor our teenagers require—reveals itself through the prism of our own subjectivity. In a certain sense, the metaphysical sky is like a giant screen onto which the inner workings of our psyche are projected. This does not mean that the transcendent realm is only a projection of our thoughts and emotions, as some philosophers have proposed. But because we cannot fully grasp the infinite with our conscious, rational minds, any notion of it we may hold is tinged with the affect of our upbringing, our preconceptions, the stories we have been told, and our own psychological state.

A Continuously Deepening Experience of the Infinite

Although the metaphysical sky described in our framework should provide an anchor for our teens, we by no means want them to see this sky as frozen and one-dimensional. Teens, who are still working to integrate the components of their personalities into a stable identity, tend to think and experience life in a dualistic way. This dualism is often projected onto the heavens. The transcendent realm can come to represent terror and punishment, either by becoming the focus of irrational fears and superstitions or by casting a dark shadow of disapproval, and thus function as a soaring, concave mirror that reflects and amplifies already existing feelings of shame and guilt.

The teenage years, which are formative in so many ways, are often used by fundamentalist religious sects as a time of intense indoctrination. The adolescent tendency toward perceiving the world dualistically suits the fundamentalist agenda well; indoctrination, when it does not spark rebellion, works to fix the teenager's metaphysical conception at this point of rigidity and polarization, where the sky appears as static, inspiring obedience and fear.

Our ambition, to the contrary, is to begin a process of dialogue with the heavens that will continue for a teenager's entire life. Instead of "fixing" its nature in a rigid definition, we want our adolescents to have a continuously deepening experience of the infinite, of an absolute that is grasped in a multidimensional way.

Much of the rebellion against spirituality and religion that was characteristic of Western intellectuals in the 19th century and in the first part of the 20th century was caused by society's inability to educate toward a more complex and open conception of the divine. There is a Hasidic story about this set in the era in which Enlightenment ideas were beginning to spread like wildfire through Eastern European Jewish communities. Exposed to the ideas of scientific rationalism, one young man found it impossible to believe anymore in the concept of God he had formulated as a child—as an awesome being with a long white beard sitting on a royal throne. Troubled, he went to ask a Hasidic Rebbe, or spiritual master, for advice. The Rebbe, intuiting the young man's state of mind, greeted him with the words: "The God you no longer believe in, I don't believe in either."

While adolescents who hold onto a narrow interpretation of belief may end up as fundamentalists, exposing them to a broad spectrum of interpretations will, at the end of the day, encourage them to make a link, allowing for a meaningful spiritual life.

How are we to guide our teens towards an open-ended relationship with the transcendent, one that will continue to develop and grow? First of all, as in other areas we have discussed, we have to try to remove the aspect of threat that can darken the sky for our teenagers. Teens can perceive fate as an irrational and demonic presence in their lives, and parents and teachers, if they are not mindful, can give power to this feeling. Sentences like "If you don't watch out, you are going to end up like so and so," and talk about divine punishment or vengeance in general, even when it is not directed toward your child, can enhance teenagers' sense of irrational powers. So can anxiety about religious observance: non-verbal or even subconscious feelings that parents or teachers convey can make a teenager feel that something terrible might happen if a particular ritual is not completed, a belief is questioned, or a taboo is broken. Our goal is for the sky to shine; we want this radiance to accompany our children and give them strength throughout their long journey in life. For this to happen, we don't have to speak necessarily about love. It is enough to remove the atmosphere of fear and threat that often sneaks in as we attempt to teach our children about transcendent notions of right and wrong. Removing threat from teenage lives is already a potent act of love. Love-talk can raise expectations that cannot be fully realized. When threat is removed, the pool of love will fill up from underground sources.

TARGETING GOD

By avoiding the anxiety that can accompany religious education, in fact by not talking much about God at all, we can avoid making the transcendent a target for rebellion. The adolescent, in search of self-definition, is always looking for such targets. Those of us who are part of a particular religious tradition or cherish specific beliefs, wish to transmit these beliefs to our children. But if a teenager senses that this transmission is freighted with concern and anxiety, if religious teachings are accompanied by an open or subliminal threat to withhold love or support from a child who rejects these beliefs, it is as if a gilded invitation to rebel has been extended. The potential tragedy in this set of circumstances is that rebellion means polarization; once again, God is "set up" to represent one side of the duality that exists within the teenage psyche, thus "freezing" God and blocking spiritual development. Our hope is that our teenagers will come to experience God as totality. Just as we hope to create a sense of continuity and internal unity in the flow of time from past to future represented by the horizontal line, so, too, we wish to allow our children to experience the transcendent as a place or entity beyond time in which all the fragments of their inner and outer world merge into oneness.

But how can faith be taught without focusing on or targeting "God"? If our children realize how important it is to us that they have faith, they will rebel. And yet is not faith of utmost importance? How can we escape this quandary?

Perhaps most importantly, we must learn to demonstrate faith rather than demanding it. The most effective way for our teens to learn about faith is by feeling the faith we have in them. We can think about it as we do a geometrical theorem in which the angles of two sides of a triangle define the angle of the third side. If we have faith in our children, and they see that we also have faith in God, they will absorb the lesson of faith in God even if it is not explicit. We need to have faith in our children's goodness, in their abilities, in their ultimate success in life. They will understand the profound inner connection between our faith in God, our faith in life, and our faith in them, and will eventually follow the stream of faith back to its source.

This won't necessarily happen instantly, although sometimes it does. We have to be ready, though, to have faith in our child's religious development as we would in a barren field that we have just begun to seed. It is even possible that our child's religious faith will awaken only when we are no longer an immediate presence in their life—in missing us, for instance, the faith that we represent will become available to them. Sometimes this process takes more than one generation, and in the end, it is our grandchildren who will ultimately inherit our faith, as they hear about us from their parents, and sense the wholeness of our personalities unimpeded by the negative interactions that sometimes mar relations with parents. In terms of transmitting faith, as in other matters, mentoring and parenting should be understood as an act of *Tikkun Olam* whose ripples reach the broadest circles of our human affiliation, not an expression of our need to allay our existential insecurity by replicating ourselves. Appreciation for other religious traditions and the idea that there is a quality of religiosity that transcends every specific expression of faith is an integral part of the children's experience in our village. It was only natural, therefore, that our dialogue with Tibetan educators led us to invite Tibetan teenagers from the Tibetan Children's Villages in India and Nepal for an extended stay at Yemin Orde. When the Tibetan teenagers came to our Sabbath prayer service and meditated as we chanted and read the Torah, we saw this as part and parcel of fostering our own spiritual development.

When I finally reached Boris, a child of Muslim and Christian lineage living on the streets of war-torn Sarajevo, what we talked about was his dream of a life in Israel. "You can rest easy," I told him before hanging up the phone. "As far as I'm concerned, you can consider your Israel dream already fulfilled." From the moment I first greeted him at the airport until his graduation ceremony several years later, Boris's unique ethnic and religious background silently played a significant role; becoming an asset and providing the glue that cemented together disparate experiences and parts of his personality. Boris eventually returned to build his life in Europe, and remained true to himself and his own original roots. His presence and the presence of others like him in our village has made me feel that we are fulfilling, in our own small way, the biblical promise that "My house will be called a house of prayer for all peoples."

We don't want to mark God for rebellion by focusing on obedience, retribution, or even love. We do, however, want to help open the channels through which our children can be guided on their journey by a living connection with the metaphysical sky above. The vector pointing upwards should rise toward a horizon in which all the fragments of a sometimes shattered existence merge into a unified whole. If we can see totality and wholeness outside ourselves, at the point where existence transcends our grasp, we will gain the ability to feel the inner unity of our own psyche and identity. Our ability to grasp ourselves as whole emanates from our ability to see the whole outside of ourselves. This is what we wish for our children—that the sky above them, the beyond which surrounds and envelops their lives, should be experienced as a place where the pieces of life's puzzle, the seeming contradictions and conflicts, co-exist in harmony. Then, as the Psalmist says, "Like an infant at his mother's breast," the act of turning toward the sky will become a moment of profound solace and comfort.

13

TIKKUN OLAM
MENDING THE WORLD

What is it that transforms a group of individuals into a community? Often, at the Yemin Orde Youth Village, it is the intrinsic drive for justice that has galvanized our youngsters into an active community. Community activism was forged through the tangible sense of the suffering of others and identification with their existential situation—and thus a feeling of participation in a shared fate. When our graduates look back on their years in our village, the motif that surfaces over and over is the way that their communal experience at Yemin Orde compensated them for the bitter lack of family and stable surroundings that they had suffered during childhood. The weakening of both the family and a sense of community in general today increases the urgency of introducing communal qualities into our schools.

Indeed, for some time now the issue of community has been an important item on the agenda of educators. Much lip service has been paid to the notion that violence, drugs, and other problems plaguing many public schools can be combated by creating a more intense sense of community.

Unfortunately, for the most part, the talk has remained talk—a flag without much wind behind it. When there is no ideological glue or intensive parental involvement binding a school together, community feeling is difficult to produce. This is true especially in large public schools whose students and their parents may have little in common except for geographical proximity. When we are talking about children from impoverished inner-city homes, or homes haunted by feelings of failure, creating community is even harder due to the sense of isolation and alienation with which many of these children have been raised. Their families' daily struggle for survival often left little energy to devote to communal affairs, and little faith in the power of association to strengthen and enrich individual lives.

Only if a school's desire to create community has the urgency of an existential need do efforts to reach this goal stand a chance of success. At Yemin Orde, despite the weak jumping-off point of many of our youths and the eclectic backgrounds they come from, we have been able to create a strong communal bond. This success is attributable, first and foremost, to our commitment to the centrality of community as a human and educational goal. True community cannot be a byproduct of something else. Although any group that comes together for a unified purpose may take on aspects of a community, a community is alive only if on some core level its life is its purpose. No matter what lofty purposes a human being is devoted to, in order to be strong and healthy, one needs to feel, at some deep foundational level, a simple joy at being alive. The same is true in terms of community; a school or other group may have many goals, but the impulse to community must be a vibrant force at the core of that school or group's life else it be perceived, rightly, as an empty motto.

Transformation of the institution into community can only come through the metamorphosis, or even the intention of metamorphosis, of at least a skeleton staff consisting of people willing to participate in the adventure of preparedness, which entails changing within.

Transforming schools into communities is important not only because doing so will bring down the level of violence and substance abuse, although it undoubtedly will. It is important because our adolescents must learn what it is to participate in the life of a community. As a society, we cannot afford to produce communal cripples, people for whom isolation, anonymity and alienation are the norm. Our teenagers must emerge from their adolescent years having found an expression for the natural human urge to belong. The taste of community that children experience during their adolescent years will whet their appetite to participate in communal life for the remainder of their days.

PERPETUALLY REINVENTED COMMUNITY

Kurt Hahn was one of the outstanding educators of the last century. Born in Germany, Hahn continued his work in England after Hitler's rise to power. I was personally introduced to his work by his sister-in-law, Lola Hahn Wahrburg, who devoted her life to saving Jewish children from the clutches of the Nazis and rehabilitating child survivors after the Holocaust. Toward the end of her long life, Wahrburg saw in Yemin Orde a continuation of her brother-in-law's educational path. Kurt Hahn believed that the schools of the future must function as communities of meaning and idealism in which the drive towards self-realization is harnessed to an overarching goal: the creation of a better world. A dynamo of ideas and activities, Hahn's fecund mind produced an array of educational initiatives including an international network of schools called the United World Colleges, and Outward Bound, the short course designed to catalyze teenage transformation. Hahn mostly focused on influencing and training children of the elite in hopes that they would later be in positions through which they could profoundly affect positive changes in society. In Yemin Orde, we have applied Hahn's idea of schools as communities of meaning to the raising of children from impoverished backgrounds and dysfunctional families.

One important principle to keep in mind in this regard is that, especially for adolescents, community is something that has to be created over and over again. Dedication to and identification with a particular community is strongest among its founders. Here in Israel we've witnessed this phenomenon in regards to the *kibbutz* movement. During the half century preceding the founding of the State, and for a decade or so afterwards, hundreds of *Kibbutzim*— collective farms, with their own schools, economies, cultures and welfare systems—were carved out of barren deserts and swamps. The founding members of the *kibbutz* movement endured enormous hardships in order to establish these communities against all odds. Often they lived under conditions of dire poverty. Ultimately, most of the *kibbutzim* thrived, and contributed enormously to the development of Israel while creating culturally vibrant and ideologically committed communities. But lo and behold, the second and third generation of Israelis born on *kibbutz* began a mass exodus from *kibbutz* life, despite having achieved a far higher standard of living than their parents or grandparents had ever dreamed possible. One of the clear lessons that emerged was that the farther removed people were from the *kibbutz's* founding, the less connected they felt to the *kibbutz* as individuals. Since they did not feel like founders, the emphasis on community was interpreted as coming at the expense of individual expression. In order to feel that they were living their own lives, many left the *kibbutz* and went to live in cities.

Perhaps for similar reasons, the Torah tells us that all the souls of Israel, including those of unborn generations to come, were present at Mount Sinai, when Israel became a community. True membership always means partaking in the moment of origin in some way.

Schools that want to be communities should take this lesson seriously. Instead of giving new students the feeling that they are joining an already established community, the school should aspire to be a community forever in formation, fundamentally changed by each new member. Every child at his or her point of entry, it should be assumed, is far from being part of a community. Especially when we are talking about those children who are emerging from traumatic childhoods, teenagers are creatures deeply absorbed in themselves. One cannot look at community as something static, as if you are adding new individuals to something that already exists, because with that mindset, the children and the community will repel each other.

With each class, it is necessary to build the consciousness of community anew. In Hebrew, the word for education is "dedication" or "inauguration." If the educator does not believe that he or she is inaugurating something new, then education is not really happening. In education we are always planting—the fruits come later. Initiating youngsters into the passionate desire for community can be accomplished only by engaging them as individuals, allowing them to feel that the magical power of the collective could not have been conjured without the potency of their unique presence.

COMMUNITY—IN THE SERVICE OF THE EGO

Most youngsters arrive in our village having felt weakened by the group to which they belong. They may have suffered from or internalized stereotypes that were tagged onto them as children of immigrants, or single-parent families, or residents in distressed, low-income neighborhoods. In order to change their concept of belonging, to open them up to community, we have to turn this notion upside down. We have to make our teenagers feel empowered by their membership in the group—empowered not as part of the group, but *as individuals* because of the group. In short, we need to create a synergy in which the group is continuously felt to be drawing its power from the individual potencies of its participants, even as it bestows upon them the blessings of its collective power.

For us at Yemin Orde, the presence of alumni is a key factor in demonstrating the power the community possesses to change the lives of individuals for the better. From their first days in our village, teenagers know that the Yemin Orde community is not an artificial construct governed by the abstract set of rules stipulating that high school lasts for four years. As described earlier, membership in our village community does not dissipate suddenly the day after graduation. Alumni remain part of the day-to-day life of the village. Our youngsters know the extent to which the Yemin Orde community and the alumni continue to give to each other long after graduation. The alumni share their lives as they pass through the army, through university, into marriage, and as they are creating their own families. Those who have succeeded share with the village adolescents both the joy and the resources that are the results of their success. Conversely, the village continues to help alumni, both financially and with our name and connections, in furthering their educations, helping them get work and generally succeeding along the paths they have chosen.

The role of alumni in reinforcing a sense of community is recognized and utilized by schools such as Harvard and Yale, Eton and Exeter. Generations of prominent and well-connected alumni keep in close contact with these schools and serve to keep us aware of its elite nature and the expected successes of its graduates. The innovation of Yemin Orde, which we believe deserves adoption on a much broader scale, is to make alumni a significant matter of concern and activity for schools that serve "weak" populations. When the youth in our village see alumni returning to celebrate their weddings, graduations from university, or attainment of the rank of officer in the army, they understand the role of community in changing the course of individual lives. It is high time that school systems serving weak populations begin reaching out to their alumni—launching intensive, continual contact with them as a way to help their current student populations. What if inner-city schools had continuous, built-in programs that served alumni by helping them to obtain scholarships, counseling them about career choices, assisting them as they look for work, celebrating their achievements and smoothing out their failures? These efforts, even if kept on a low flame for lack of resources, would go a long way toward creating an authentic sense of community at the school, as well as modeling trustworthy examples of hope and fulfillment for the future. It is our experience that the investment of time, funding and energy that such a program entails will eventually be justified by the quality of human lives it fosters as well as quantitative economic returns.

One strategy for enhancing awareness of the advantages of membership in a community is to consciously create a broader network of people with whom the school is associated. Our village has a number of "adopted" parents and grandparents, older figures who represent stability, wisdom and connections to the higher strata of Israeli society. Rachel Rabin, the martyred Prime Minister's sister and one of the early founders of *Kibbutz Manara* on the Lebanese border, is an occasional visitor to our village. So are artists, architects, businesspeople and other public figures. Our youngsters absorb that their village has a network of people that care about them and the village, and that can be a resource later in life. This strategy can be used successfully by any school. At its core, it sends the message that belonging is not a prison but rather a springboard from which one can reach wider and wider circles of affiliation.

Struggles provide an ideal context in which individuals can perceive their own powers emerging as they participate in communal efforts. Schools constantly need to make efforts, against all odds, to attain more resources, better funding, the expansion of facilities or the creation of opportunities for their alumni. Instead of hiding these struggles, students should be made to feel part of them, as if they personally have a stake in the outcomes. Last summer, a group of our youngsters were not paid as they had been promised for jobs they had completed. Yemin Orde took up their cause, and after several rounds of letters, phone calls, and threats of legal action, we managed to help recover their wages. Just as importantly, we let the other young people know exactly what we were doing all the way through, including them in the excitement of the battle and reminding them of the value inherent in being part of a community.

ROUTINE AND BUREAUCRACY: ENEMIES OF COMMUNITY

Where possible, schools should seek opportunities to fight for causes that are consistent with their ideology and stand a chance of galvanizing the student population. Think of it as another form of team sports, where the stakes don't involve winning games, but changing reality. And just as team sports are opportunities for individual talents and willpower to shine within the context of a larger group, so are public campaigns. However, there is one important difference: the battles in which the school engages must be real, and not games. How far we have drifted from the original experience of life in rural villages can be measured by our belief that education can take place in a protected bubble in which words and simulation are the primary educational tools. One cannot establish and reinforce community through simulation. The extent to which adolescents perceive the struggle we involve them in as authentic and not masturbatory will determine how deeply engaged they become in said struggle, and how thoroughly they experience a sense of belonging.

This, incidentally, is the secret to creating a community that is always in the process of being created, so that every teen feels close to the origins. One must consciously allow the facade of stability that institutions work so hard to put in place to be knocked out of whack, at least a little bit. Of course, this approach must be balanced by the reassurance that things will turn out alright in the end—adolescents should ultimately live with a feeling of protection rather than existential threat. But disturbing balances and asking teenagers to help influence a situation in which the stakes are real is a crucial step in awakening their hidden powers and fostering a sense of agency within a communal setting.

Indeed, routine is the enemy of community, especially where adolescents are concerned. Adolescence is short, and we have a very limited amount of time as educators in which to convey the essence of belonging to our children. If they do not experience the rhythm of community as a pulse of life, as something with its own urgencies and surprises, they will retreat into their own private world. Or into the world of their peers, fed by a subculture that feels exciting because it appears to be constantly under threat. Only by continuously fighting, struggling, and challenging the status quo can a community avoid ossification and deadening.

Bureaucracy is thus the other great foe of community. Where one is strong, the other has no real foothold. To whatever extent possible, bureaucracy should be reduced or eliminated. To the extent it cannot be, then both its procedures and its logic should be made transparent. Adolescents should be taught the reasons that we have forms, procedures and hierarchies so that they understand that bureaucracy, where it must exist, is not a matter of principle but of function—that it serves community, rather than the other way around.

ACCESSIBLE AUTHORITY

This attitude toward bureaucracy should be built into the physical environment of schools. The architecture of schools, particularly their physical layouts, can serve to either magnify or reduce alienation and fear. In our village, there is no main administration building. The administrative operations needed to run each section are carried out in the area itself. When there is a separate administration building that concentrates much of the institution's power in one location, this broadcasts a kind of "Big Brother" image, as if the administrators are organizing life without being part of life. It is important that the administration participates in the flow of life, and that children clearly see this.

There are many schools where the headmaster or director is

reachable only by navigating a long hall and then making it past the barricade of a secretary's office. Instead, educators should be cultivating accessibility by creating an environment of availability. Everything about the architecture of the school and the placement of offices should encourage openness and convey a sense of transparency. Youngsters in our village learn soon after arriving that even when I am in a meeting, and the secretary is unwilling to interrupt me, they have recourse if they really need to see me. They can walk around the back of my office and knock on the window. Besides concretely demonstrating that my intention is to remain as accessible to them as possible, the back-window knock shows that, in our community, relationship takes precedence over rules. Formalities exist, but when the emotional intimacy that nourishes community is present, there is always a back way around them. This also serves to reinforce the youngsters' moral judgment at a very crucial juncture in their development. Although rules and laws are generally to be followed, one's judgment is relevant in assessing their validity when they seem to conflict with urgent human values—in this case, the preference of relationship over administrative rigidity.

Authority that is inaccessible, on the other hand, is an enemy of community; it reinforces a fear of separation and abandonment. Teenagers need to feel that the people who hold power in their lives can be reached without formality or delay. Teenagers should ideally be able to talk to their counselors, educators, and the director of the village or school without an appointment when necessary, and about whatever they wish to discuss.

We have learned over the years to try and use our youngsters' requests and desires as educational opportunities. Kids, of course, do not need to get everything they ask for. We can say no, or the request can become part of a more complicated negotiation. But even if the final answer is no, for the child, the fact that he or she has had the chance to discuss the request is of tremendous significance. This opportunity should be built into the environment. In the short term, the youngster engages in an intimate discourse rather than being thrown back against a wall of frustration. The long-lasting fruit is the creation of a personality able to make demands on itself, provided the young person has good reason to see the adult authority as encircled together with him or her in an extended sense of self.

One further way in which we make village authorities available to students is a concerted effort to include adolescent representation in the leadership of the school. In order to be effective, though, this representation must be real; otherwise it will only increase feelings of distrust in light of the gap between statement and actual partnership. Student representatives should be allowed to understand school politics and finances, and when there are problems, even scandals, they should hear about it. It is amazing to see how our board members take on the role of educators due to the presence of our adolescents at meetings. When the village's accountants share and explain documents to our youngsters, they create a different kind of attitude toward our organization, property and financial commitments. This attitude is one of inner coherence between our administrative operations and our educational goals, and it is something we seek to transmit to even the newest youngster arriving in our village. We also want the children to be able to understand that administrators are not invulnerable, and are prone to error and possibly even misdeed. We want them to be able to talk about the personalities involved in institutional politics, because those murky crosscurrents created when discussion flows into gossip, like salty and fresh water in an estuary, produce the lifeblood of communal feeling.

We do not want anyone in the school or the administration to be a placard, known only by his or her function. Secretaries, educators, cooks and administrators all have to have a human face. We want our village to be the repudiation of Kafka's universe of alienation. This means that the community, including the children, needs to have some window into the intimacy of our staff—

their past, problems and challenges. I make a practice of taking new youngsters at our village on a tour of my house, showing them at least a small opening into the inner dimensions of my life. Then, even when I am acting in my role as director, they feel that they can see at least a little bit beyond that role into the totality of my life.

CLANDESTINE ARTERIES AND STOPPING LIFE

It is people who create community. If schools are serious about this task, then the heads of the system must value and honor not only those educators that bring academic excellence and honors to the school, but also those few people that are agents of unity and community—they are as important and significant as the great teachers of math. Just as all sorts of knowledge and information and gossip flows through the system in an informal way, so can communality—if these agents exist. Similarly, the presence of alumni, as in the case of Yemin Orde, provides a connective tissue linking teenagers and their teaching and administrative staff.

We have an opportunity to use the same currents that carry gossip and news of scandal as a channel to infuse the system with a feeling of community, but we must make a conscious effort to do so. The opened windows of intimacy weaken the need for a separate youth subculture based on categorical disdain for the world of adults. Our goal should be to bring the culture and subculture of the school closer together, so that a single network of arteries carries the buzz of information and gossip to the community as a whole, as if it were one body. Communities must suffer the bad as well as celebrate the good.

Recently, two of our beloved teachers died of cancer within a single year. Not long afterwards, the 7-year-old daughter of one of our village's central educational figures was murdered in a terrorist attack. A feeling that our village was under the sway of some kind of curse engulfed all of us. The reverse has also happened, where a string of awards and outstanding successes of our graduates creates a wave of communal uplifting of which every individual feels a part.

Along with these informal arteries, whose significance cannot be exaggerated, we have created other channels for disseminating information. Chief among these is the village's cable television channel, which broadcasts roughly edited personal stories, alumni success stories, and the stories of our ongoing struggles, as well as birthdays and other information—all to underscore and emphasize the synergetic interplay between community and the individual.

Misdeeds, and the shame they may produce, can be another powerful force for constituting community. At Yemin Orde, whenever there is an event that shames us—violence or threat, for example—we stop life. We do not let things go on as usual, and routine is broken. The music playing on the village loudspeakers in the dining hall is silenced. Even classes are interrupted. Because we are a community, because we are all connected, and because something has happened that negates the essence of community, life cannot go on as usual. Just as on television, "breaking news" interrupts the regularly scheduled programs.

Several years ago, a video player was stolen from one of the village common rooms. I immediately stopped classes and cancelled all extracurricular activities. We organized the young people into discussion groups and explained that life in the village would not resume as normal until the crisis in trust that the theft of public property had created was resolved. After several hours, a note was found in the synagogue, posted on the most sacred space in the village, the Holy Ark where the Torahs are stored. The note gave instructions that led to the recovery of the video player in a city a hundred miles to the south of our village.

Many times the communal atmosphere created in response to a "crime" can lead to its solution. For the "thief," listening in as a respected member of the village community to discussions about various aspects of what may have led our still-anonymous perpetrator to engage in such an act helped that youth to reflect on the deed from a different perspective. The youngster was able to see their "crime" as an aberration of their substantive and permanent identity as a member of the Yemin Orde community.

In taking measures that stop the normal flow of life, I hope to create a memory and understanding that will last for the rest of our teenagers' lives. "Were you ever in a place where there was violence?" I hear a voice asking one of our teens later in life. "Yes, I was. And life stopped, because I was in a community, and communities cannot tolerate violence." The message I want to convey is that as long as we act as a community, the flow of life in our village continues. But when the intrinsic norms without which a community cannot exist are disturbed, an emergency is declared, almost as if life itself has been threatened.

As in every instance, judgment must be exercised in this regard. Sometimes, stopping the life of the community is what a teenager intends with his or her outrageous or threatening behavior. One of our teens once attempted to hang herself from the branch of a tree, although at a time and in a manner that insured that she would be cut down in time. An event as serious as this might warrant stopping the flow of life, but in this case, I judged that it would also feed this young woman's feeling that self-destructive acts were the best way to get the attention of the entire community focused on her. As such, we emphasized the concept of "tikuun" without "collective guilt." We worked with children in small discussion groups, in which the adult/educator allowed the kids to talk, to express themselves and offer up various explanations for what the young girl had done. The discussions focused on the motivations behind the act. Multiple possible reasons emerged, and different kids identified with different motivations. Some kids identified with the motivation of "self-victimizing" while others identified with a "special need to get everyone's attention." Then, by emphasizing one of the motifs, that of the young girl's loneliness, we were able to draw practical conclusions: this loneliness is something we can all help alleviate, or fix ("Tikkun"), and we have a responsibility to prevent an individual from being isolated.

MEDIATING THE WORLD

Part of what creates a community is its relationship to other communities or groups. A community has to have an extended sense of belonging. That which binds us to each other also binds us to others outside our immediate group, and these widening circles of identification reinforce our primary communal identity. Yemin Orde identifies with all groups whose values are humanistic, and who combine an authentic interest in holiness or spirituality with a commitment to pluralism. And yet we are still a community unto ourselves. By learning to distinguish between various shades and forms of group identity, our teens hone on the subtleties of communal feeling.

At Yemin Orde, the outside world is constantly penetrating and interacting with the world of our youth. As these lines are written, we are hosting refugee children from Guinea Conakry, who saw their parents slaughtered in ethnic warfare and made it across the continent of Africa to the Israeli border. Arrested for crossing illegally into the country, Yemin Orde told the police we would take responsibility for these children. One of the rewards for us is that the teens at Yemin Orde have the opportunity to hear, and respond to, these children's story. The sense of identification and involvement in the fate of these children broadens the horizons of our adolescents' life.

It is important to us that the commercial media not be the exclusive mediator of the stories of suffering and survival coming to us from the world outside. The media is a source of information, but it is as a community that we explore and interpret the information—as if at a village council. Family meetings in which issues are discussed and the possibility of action explored are a critical tool nowadays for providing the sense of permeability and life within the stability of the family circle that teenagers need. While computers and television are certainly legitimate sources of information, too often today they are considered private domains, with each member of the family "consuming" the news from the outside world individually. Instead, the information brought by the news media, like a messenger arriving in a village from places near or far, should be discussed and digested within the intimate public space that defines the familial connection. This is part of the "translation" we need to make, in which we adopt and adapt key elements of the lost village.

Institutions, like some families, have a tendency to organize themselves, consciously or unconsciously, in a way that provides first and foremost for their own survival over time. This means that institutions, for the most part, prefer predictability to surprise and control to flexibility. Especially in residential education campuses, in which children live and learn 24/7, the institutional drive toward predictability and control runs counter to the teenager's need to feel the flow of life. Teenagers need to be part of a living community, organized around the life of its members, not an abstract institution whose basic commitment is to its own self-preservation. To the extent that teenagers feel that the place they are living is devoid of an authentic pulse of life, but instead geared towards moving its charges through a set of predetermined hoops, they will experience institutional life as prison. In one way or another, they will try to escape; either inwardly, through emotional withdrawal, or outwardly, in emphatic rebellion.

THE BELLY OF JONAH'S WHALE

As part of reconstructing an inner sense of home for our children, we have scattered womb-like structures throughout the Village where small groups of children can sit together and talk in their native language. Our "wombs" are round shacks made of wood and branches in which we have hung enlarged photos depicting everyday life in the lands they have left behind. Our aim and hope is that every time youngsters gather in these spaces, they step out with slightly more insight into themselves and the processes they are going through than when they entered.

Among the staff, we have given this experience the code name "Jonah's Whale," thus attributing a broader significance and context to the natural urge of the children to group together in an intimacy whose contours they themselves have chosen. In our tradition, the biblical whale that swallows Jonah as he attempts to escape from his mission and destiny becomes a refuge for incubating insight and energies that later enable him to save the entire civilization of Nineveh. The formation of youth subculture groups can too often and too easily take a destructive course, largely because the unarticulated threatened response of adults becomes a self-fulfilling prophecy. By making an effort to transform our attitudes we can forestall this negative result. We can create a genuinely positive association through these mini-communities, even when we feel worried or threatened by our teenager's modes of bonding to peers. This will assure us a place in the picture instead of guaranteeing our exclusion.

> I am reminded of one particular group of teenage immigrants from several Middle Eastern countries who used their sessions in the womb-like havens to talk about their futures. Like other teenagers, they used their seclusion to express themselves in ways they were uncomfortable doing in the clear light of day. This might well have included smoking, using rough language and analyzing the virtues of the opposite sex.

Yet ultimately, these youngsters transformed their "havens" into breeding grounds for idealistic musings about the future, a la *Dead Poets Society*. As in the story of Jonah, they emerged from regressive confinement in a dark place with a new trajectory, if not a sense of mission. In the end, romanticizing and fantasizing in the warm darkness about a bright future turned into an actual plan. Impressed by their resolve to try to create a future together, and their desire to learn more about life in Israel, we arranged to travel with them to the Galilee region. At some point on our journey we reached a hilltop near Nazareth that was now abandoned, although two shelters and several wooden shacks still remained from a previous attempt at settlement. Why had the buildings been abandoned? Could another group of people succeed in bringing life to this hilltop? A fiery discussion erupted. "Why not?" they exclaimed, "Test us! We will make a paradise out of this place! One day we will bring our parents to live with us here." I clearly remember Yossi, one of the teens, pointing to a clump of rocks, and saying, "That's where the bank is going to be." "And over there," said Benny, "the movie theatre is going to stand."

Almost twenty years later, in a PBS documentary about Yemin Orde, some of these same graduates were interviewed in their beautiful homes on that same hilltop, as their own children played around them. They had succeeded beyond my hopes. Today, Hoshayah, the community they founded, is a thriving village of 250 well-established families. Reminiscing about the founding of Hoshaya, the graduates retrospectively attribute their ability to turn a desolate site into a place bursting with life to the thread of promise that was woven throughout the process they had lived through since their arrival in Yemin Orde. From the vantage point of adulthood, our graduates remembered the womb-like spaces in which their dreams had been kindled.

Instead of fearing, and thus negating, the teenage urge to group together in places of refuge from the all-seeing eyes of the adults, we subtly suggested to our teenagers the "Jonah's whale" option. Because, again, the warmth and intimacy of teenage bonding can bear seeds resulting in the unexpected excitement and fulfillment of true accomplishment.

An Unmovable Platform

One important principle we aim to instill in our children from day one, is that their existence at Yemin Orde is not contingent. This principle is built into the very architecture of our village. Whereas in many boarding situations children are housed within a complex that also contains classrooms and laboratories, at Yemin Orde we are careful to separate the residential area, which represents living, from the school, which represents academic achievement. We have wholeheartedly endorsed this separation despite the distinct and sometimes even contemptuous negative reactions of bureaucratic and academic echelons, who are rigidly locked into their surety that formal education should dominate all else in the children's lives.

The walk between home, on the western slope of the village, and the school on its eastern side, takes more than a few minutes, and one area cannot be seen from the other. We want our children to understand clearly that success or failure at school will not impact their membership in the Yemin Orde community. This policy is based on the conviction that in the long run, the distinct separa-tion between home and school, when it does not supplant the mes-sage that performing well at school is still important to us, actually helps foster academic excellence. In no way should we allow home to be perceived as merely a branch of school. The delicate balance between encouraging and helping our children academically, while underlining the separation between school and home helps produce youth with a capacity and enthusiasm for learning.

The map of Yemin Orde is a metaphor for what, as parents and educators, we need to strive to give to our teenagers, namely a world that is both bounded and whole. Bounded because the opposite, abandonment, is borderless; the dread of infinite drifting. There needs to be an element of isolation in order to provide the contours of a home. That is why we are insistent on separating home and school. Teens need an environment in which their fragmented psyches, stretched between past and future, childhood and maturity, can find a depiction of wholeness. They need boundaries in order to provide them with at least a provisional sense of solidity, a platform where they can safely stand and assemble the fragments of their life into a unified whole.

Messianic Eyes to See What Is Real

But wholeness cannot be created by boundaries alone. The presence of a significant adult figure able to see the potential wholeness that exists in a teenager already, who can see beyond their current fragmented identity, is crucial. In many cultures, eyes are understood to be more than passive receptacles of sight, but to have a deeper power that emanates from them, that can bring blessing or cause damage, depending on the intent of the seer.

In Jewish folklore, some of the righteous are said to have "Messianic eyes," meaning they can see how others would look in a redeemed world, when their best potential has been realized. We have to train ourselves to look at our adolescents with this kind of eyes. Without the transforming presence of adults who are able to give these youngsters a sense that they are responding to them not only as they are now, but also as they someday will be, boundaries might quickly become a prison from which they would push to escape. Only the living presence of an adult "guide" who sees the teenager through the prism of an inner roadmap can create a world that is both secure and dynamic enough to allow the adolescent journey of exploration to continue.

We constantly need to remind ourselves that in previous generations, the path to adulthood was more or less clearly defined. Firm models existed that provided distinct goals around which teenagers could form their identities. The gentleman, the farmer, the nobleman, the warrior, the scholar and the priest were all archetypes towards which a well-trodden path already existed. It's true that often the choices an adolescent faced were constricting in the extreme. The son of serfs could not grow up to be a nobleman. Class structures were very rigid. And for women, in particular, the kinds of roles toward which they could aspire was even more limited, no matter what class they came from.

And yet we do not need to idealize the past in order to be fully aware of the problematic nature of the present. Today's world is filled with so much uncertainty that few of us can guarantee our children's long-term future. What we can do is to ensure our adolescents that they have a firm platform to stand on, and that this platform will eventually connect them to the next stage in life, the next platform. Here at Yemin Orde, we have tried to take advantage of our ability to shape the environment in order to create a world that reflects the totality of our youths' concerns; that addresses their depth dimension as well as their physical or intellectual needs. Not every educator can shape the environment in the way we do here. Yet an adult who plays a significant role in a teenager's life can help provide a virtual platform, a place where an adolescent can feel secure and relax into living, because all of him or her is being seen. It is only by relating to many dimensions of a child's life that we can help catalyze inner change in our relationship with our teenagers. This kind of change will allow the adolescent to locate their strengths and compensate for their weaknesses, to gather and use all the powers that life has placed under their command.

THE PADANI FAMILY: *FIGHTING FOR A HOME*

The Padani family lived in little more than a shack on the outskirts of Southern Tel Aviv. The mother and father had arrived in Israel from an Islamic country in the Middle East with neither means nor education—they only had each other. The nearly ruined apartment they found soon after reaching Israel was part of an abandoned building, and it took everything they had to make it into a home. Both worked hard at menial jobs and every year seemed to bring another child, until finally the family numbered 14 children. During one of Mr. Padani's frequent attempts to expand the living area of his family's home, an iron support bar fell on his leg, permanently crippling him.

Now unable to fend for their children, the Padanis became dependent on welfare. The younger children were taken away from their home, which was considered in danger of collapse. Three of the teenagers were placed in our village. Angry over having been forced to leave home, the three young sons refused to cooperate and lashed out against our counselors and the other youngsters. All the attempts we made to bring them into the life of the village and integrate them into daily activities failed. The date that the Tel Aviv municipality had set for the destruction of their childhood home approached and overshadowed all our attempts to channel them towards new endeavors.

At the basis of the Yemin Orde community lies the axiom that an individual's plight is the plight of all of us. In this case in particular, the Padani brothers' crisis resonated with our youngsters—the concrete threat that their family home would be razed served as a potent metaphor for the destruction of home that most of our youth had experienced themselves in one way or another. With our encouragement, the day of the proposed house razing became a central focus for the youngsters in the Village. The case had reached the newspapers, and our teens, even those who rarely read unless they had to, hungrily devoured and compared the different accounts. They learned that the Padanis, despite their poverty, were a loving and unified family. The kids sought out knowledge of the legalities governing house destruction and whether the situation might possibly be reversed. As the date of the bulldozers approached, the whole village felt, mentally and emotionally, that they had become "The House of Padani." It was also clear, without our having to say so, that if the Padanis were left homeless, Yemin Orde Youth Village would be their home for the time being.

When the day came, the Padani brothers arrived to protect their home accompanied by four busloads of their newly found extended family. Looking back, I still ask myself whether it was responsible of me, as an educator, to go ahead with the children's plan to oppose the ruling of the court. I knew, though, that we had to be faithful to our guiding principle regarding the purity and power of the adolescent quest for justice, which we see as an outburst from the depth of their humanity, and not merely a developmental stage as categorized by one theory or another. Words alone will not suffice in situations where only deeds can reaffirm such basic beliefs and conceptions.

Needless to say, we ensured our youngsters' safety in the face of the bulldozers and police, though our hearts occasionally skipped a beat out of concern that this real-life drama could veer out of control. Fortunately, the youths' efforts led to a delay in the home-razing, which gave the welfare authorities time to engage in a search for a decent alternative housing solution— eventually finding the apartment where the parents live today. After this experience, the Padani brothers' attitude towards the village totally changed, and the village collectively felt a deep sense of achievement.

THE PASSION FOR JUSTICE AS A PURE FLAME

This anecdote from the life of our village is one of the more extreme manifestations of the power of the teenage pursuit of justice. Yet on the whole, teenagers' passion for justice is no weaker than their drive for excitement and adventure. Youth movements, which understand this passion well, are able to channel this energy into campaigns that help shape the character of adolescents while catalyzing social change. Israel itself—its Kibbutz movement and its defense force—was built through the power of young people's desire to create a new world based on the pillars of justice.

As we know, a toddler learning to talk experiences the plasticity of language, playing with sounds and meanings as adults rarely do. The process of acquiring language for the first time brings children back to the very roots and origins of language. Perhaps this is why young children have the capacity to learn several languages at once. Similarly, for adolescents, the necessity of finding a place within a society of peers, forging an identity, and eventually choosing a direction within society at large brings them back to the roots of society, and thus to what could be defined as a natural obsession with justice. The question of justice, of the way things *should* be, is at the heart of the matter when we are dealing with the basic material of society's formation.

If an adult's sense of identity is centered around that part of the self that has been actualized, the teenager's identity is connected more directly with a sense of their own potential; "I am who I can imagine myself to be." Questions of justice, of the fairness of life and society, are intimately related to teenagers' ability to imagine their potential realized. In an unjust society, a particular individual's possibilities for fulfillment are often blocked by a power structure that favors those with entrenched privileges, while in a perfectly just society every teenager will ultimately receive the chance to realize their self and their talents. None of us yet live in such a perfect society, thus the teenage quest for justice may seem a forgivable aberration.

However, if we perceive the teenager's concern with justice as a pure and unadulterated flame rising spontaneously from within, we may feel this flame rekindled within ourselves. The linguist Noam Chomsky theorized that children have an innate ability to learn language; that what he termed the "deep structure" of grammar and syntax are built into the human brain, waiting to be activated. When working with teenagers it often seems as if the desire to see justice done—within the family, society, and in the world—is built into the structure of the human soul, and bursts out passionately during the course of adolescence.

Despite its potentially volatile nature, the adolescent obsession with justice should be seen as a gift of inestimable value by parents and educators. Part of our goal in raising adolescents should be to recognize, preserve and develop their craving for justice and their wish to make the world a better place. This aspiration is already present in an intrinsic fashion. What hope does the world have if this characteristic, instead of being cherished and encouraged, is allowed to wither, or worse yet, is treated with disdain? When the burning passion for justice with which young people are endowed is repeatedly dampened or extinguished, cynicism often takes its place.

This flame of passion for justice—*Tikkun Olam*—that burns within our teenagers' souls deserves our attention, protection and active guidance.

KEEPING THE FLAME ALIVE

While some of the qualities that characterize adolescence need to follow their natural course and disappear before maturity can be reached, the intrinsic quest for justice is not one of these. Carrying the flame of justice into adulthood can ease the burden of unfinished business and emotional wounds by shifting us from our egocentricity and marking our individuality with transcendent significance. To the extent that the years following adolescence involve a struggle for personal success and survival, they can bend people and make them adjust to a crooked reality, thus causing them to abandon the dream of justice as unattainable. Fuel to stoke their passion for justice must be stored for young people during their formative years. This fuel is accumulated by involving teenagers in an existential discourse formed through exposing and engaging them in efforts to right wrongs and see that justice is done, and supporting their actions to make the world a better place. It is important that teens experience the taste of at least partial victory or success in these efforts. This taste provides proof that the attainment of justice does not go against all the odds; that the utopian dream of a just world can actually penetrate the vessels of everyday reality.

Utopian dream, you may ask? What about the destructive and anti-social behaviors, that make a bitter mockery of justice, that are often so characteristic of adolescence? Let's go back, for instance, to the phenomenon of theft in our village, when youth who had less stole from those who had more. More than once, teenagers who confessed to stealing explained their misdeeds as no less than acts of justice—efforts simply to redistribute wealth. However misguided the execution, much of teenage anger is connected to a highly developed sense of justice—educators are perceived as unfairly favoring other students, or parents other siblings—and provocations are committed as vigilante acts of protest. These acts are usually accompanied by a feeling of helplessness. When the elements that should be part of the teenage world—a sense of the past and future, ideals, and so forth—are absent, adolescents will apply their instinct for justice to the shrunken world in which they find themselves. The consequence, often, is that the school or the family itself will become a devastated battlefield.

Battles as Educational Tool

Broadening horizons toward which an adolescent can sally forth may not seem like a magical formula. Yet our experience with educational programs geared to engage teenagers in ethical issues and questions of moral judgment is that they diminish phenomena such as theft. No longer are teens as prone to distorting moral logic until their egotistical ends justified the means. Just reading the newspaper together with teens and inviting debate on ethical issues is a good start. Trying to change the world, through "battles" or projects, big or small, is even better. They can take aim at interest groups, bureaucracies, an unjust system, or simply indifference. The "battle" could be forcing the city to make wheelchair-accessible restrooms in a public park, or it could mean getting a hammer and nails and building a ramp on your own.

Battles are excellent educational tools, because they are focused, involve positions that need to be examined, interpreted and articulated, and because they create a circle of togetherness that includes adults and teenagers. Letter writing campaigns, demonstrations, lobbying elected officials, information gathering—any forum in which you can involve your adolescents in fighting for a cause that both of you consider just will have a powerful impact as an educational tool. So will feeding the hungry, visiting the sick or lonely, and reading to the blind—especially when such activities are accompanied by a discussion of why they are necessary and what society can do in order to better take care of those who are in need.

REAL-LIFE ENCOUNTERS

As you can probably tell by now, at Yemin Orde there is almost always some kind of "battle" going on, often pitting the Village against some outside force. In these campaigns, we may end up appearing before a judge. Sometimes our fights make it all the way to the Supreme Court. One never knows what the educational outcome of such real-life encounters will be. For example, we recently went through the final stage of a battle against an artist's colony called Ein Hod, which is our next-door neighbor. Ein Hod decided to set aside some land on the hill directly below the Village for use as a community cemetery. My intuition was that this was bad for our village. My reasoning was that the last thing our youngsters should have to see when they look just beyond the borders of our village is death. No small percentage of the youth living in our village are orphans or have been abandoned by one parent or another. For many, our Yemin Orde is the first experience of stability that they have had in a lifetime of uncertainty. I worried that the sight of a cemetery just outside the fence delineating the village would send a negative message: *death is what is waiting for you beyond the safe haven of Yemin Orde.* At the very least, I felt, Yemin Orde should have been consulted before Ein Hod made its final plans.

We learned as much as we could about how to fight what we considered the improper use of land. This in itself was a revelation for many of the kids; that they can use their sense of justice to shape their environment! That they are not simply passive bystanders who must accept the decisions made for them by inaccessible and impersonal authorities! That they have the right to make themselves heard! Eventually, the case went to court. Yemin Orde staff attended the court case along with a group of representatives of the children who offered testimony to the judge. One result of our legal battle was that everyone in our village was suddenly touching the motif of death. What is usually a taboo subject, one that often fascinates and scares teenagers, became an open topic of conversation, and thus lost some of its power to frighten.

Eventually, we lost the case. But we managed to find lessons even in the loss. During a group-dynamics session on the lawn, I heard one teen saying to another that it was actually a nice thing that people from Ein Hod wanted to be buried near where they had lived. It meant, in this young person's eyes, that death was a continuation of life, not an absolute disruption. So in the end, even battles that are lost can turn into a source of insights, as the debate surrounding them builds a teenager's confidence in her ability to understand and interact with the world around herself.

Acts of Heroism

Involving teens in recognizing and rewarding acts of heroism in the fight against evil also helps to affirm and reinforce their innate sense of justice. This past fall, an Israeli Arab teenager, about the same age as our students, succeeded in foiling a Palestinian suicide bomber who was on his way to blow himself up along with as many people as he could take with him. By chance, the young Israeli Arab, who is from a town 40 miles or so from our village, sat next to the suicide bomber as they waited for a bus in the Hadera-bound station. In order to make room for himself as he sat down, he picked up the bomber's knapsack. It felt suspiciously heavy. He had a sudden hunch that his fellow traveler might be about to commit mass murder. Calmly, he borrowed the suicide bomber's cell phone, claiming that he had to tell his father he would be late, walked a few feet away and called the police. When the police arrived to check the story, the bomb went off, killing the suicide bomber and the policeman and injuring the Israeli Arab teen as he attempted to run for refuge, but taking many fewer lives than if he had succeeded in embarking on the bus.

Helped by a generous donor, we turned this story into a lesson that our teens would remember by "raising a flag," to transform the incident into a potent symbol for justice and good. First, in an open discussion with our teenagers, we decided that the flowers sent by the Israeli President and the chocolates sent by the Prime Minister were not enough to show the appreciation that this young man's heroic act deserved. Our youngsters visited him in the hospital. At a ceremony in his hometown attended by village residents, we presented him with a check that we hoped would help him pay for the rest of his education. Later, he slept over in our village and we "adopted" him as an honorary member of our community. The message folded into our gift to him had several layers. By paying special attention to this young man, we showed that we honor those who put ethics above ethnic loyalties, and that we value the signs of hope that tell us that Jews and Arabs can save each other as well as kill each other. We tried to demonstrate that acts of heroism are important both in and of themselves and because they inspire others. And we showed that, as a community, we are given the opportunity to magnify the power of goodness by lending it our attention and expressing our identification and gratitude.

We try to continue nourishing stories like this over an extended period of time. In this case, we will continue to follow this young man's recovery and progress, and will find more occasions to appreciate his ethical choice in placing the value of human life over all other considerations. The story of his act and of how it moved us will become part of the story of the village, part of our tradition, and thus part of the story of each teenager living here.

REAL STRUGGLES MEND HEARTS

It is possible to take advantage of many different kinds of situations in order to introduce teenagers to the process of fighting for what is right. Sometimes, you don't even necessarily need to be right in order to turn a conflict into a learning experience. In my early years here, the village did not have a proper sewage system, or the money to have such a system installed. The Israeli Society for the Protection of Nature sued us because sewage flowing from the village was polluting a fresh water stream in the valley below. The court subpoena outlining the case against us was posted on the central billboard and immediately became the talk of the village.

While some of the village teenagers rallied to the banner we had raised, others could be heard taking a cynical stance. "So what if the village is being sued? I could care less," or "Why doesn't the village get one of our supporters to pay for the sewage pipes?"

Even these responses to the village's distress counted, for they brought to the surface feelings of abandonment that teenagers most often keep hidden. When adolescents identify a real struggle—not a theoretical debate about issues or an educational simulation, but an actual conflict or threat—it subtly touches their scars and allows their exposure to the light of day. By saying "I could care less," a teenager is joining the discussion on justice in a way that is beyond the discourse on good and evil. What the teenager really means by "I could care less" is "Look at me. Do you think I was given an equal opportunity in life?" or "Who will compensate me for the suffering I have lived through?" "Unless and until I am compensated for my pain," these teenagers are saying, "I have no interest in your campaigns." They thus signal their withdrawal into their own shrunken niche.

These conflicts afford teenagers the opportunity to express feelings that might otherwise be buried deep inside. Within the context of a real conflict, when the stakes are real, authentic feelings sitting dormant within the teenager are activated and the opportunity for mending of the heart is created. This is especially true when teenagers who initially express cynicism are eventually pulled into the conflict, and come to understand that it is possible for justice to have its day; to win, or at least to take part in a fair struggle. Even when kids stay on the sidelines and watch, it gives them a chance, in an indirect and semi-conscious way, to work on their own feelings of having been victimized. On several occasions since my arrival at the village, the atmosphere created during the communal pursuit of justice has allowed teenagers to open up and reveal their stories of victimization, including the sexual molestation that some experienced as children in institutional homes.

In the case of the spilled sewage, fighting back against our accusers became an exercise in value-laden education a la John Dewey. We studied the maps of the area, the geological makeup of the region, the legal claims against us, the rules of court procedure, and our possible lines of legal defense. We went as a group to talk to the Society for the Protection of Nature, and learned that it was not us who they were after. They were really using their attack on us as a strategy that would force government authorities to take action in regulating sewage flow and preventing pollution. A threat—"The Village is being sued"—thus transformed into a much more complex situation.

When we eventually went to court, one of our teenagers, a young Ethiopian Jewish woman, asked for permission to speak. "You see," she said to the judge, "Most of our money comes from donations for specific buildings or projects, which bear the name of the donor." Here she was fudging a little bit, as our buildings are named after inspirational heroes like Maimonides, Immanuel Kant and Martin Luther King, not after our donors. "What rich person is going to donate money for a sewage pipe?" The judge and the courtroom erupted in laughter. In the end, we were forced to pay a small fine. But the greater reward was that several of our young people were inspired, by this and other battles, and through their exposure to the legal system during this case, to become lawyers. In fact, two of them became the first attorneys from the Ethiopian immigrant community.

Is our tendency to protect children from the battles in which we are involved justified? On the whole, we should not give children the feeling that the struggles we are engaged in are mysterious and beyond the ability of children to understand, When we have trouble in our village, such as financial difficulties, it is not only the bookkeeping staff who knows and feels involved. In general, we try to create an atmosphere of financial transparency in the village. We want the children to feel the vulnerability of adults just as they feel our strength. I think that this is not a bad practice for families as well. Whether in disputes with the neighbors, employers, or other family members, parents should explain the parameters and stakes of the battle and should open a discussion about both the ethical implications of the conflict and the strategies that could be pursued. Don't children, at the end of the day, almost always know about these battles anyway? Parents should act as buffers, as shock absorbers, protecting children from the raw and ugly aspects of conflict. But they should not expect to be silencers or censors.

Involving our teenagers in the struggles that engage us brings them into the circle of real life, like people their age were before the industrial revolution. It also affords us the opportunity to raise our own standards of conflict. Instead of acting out of hurt and anger, educators who consciously include teenagers in their battles will have to clarify their stance in ethical terms in order to explain them to the children, and to modify their positions if that is what is called for. We can allow our desire to fuel our adolescent's sense of justice guide us in restoring the sharpness of our own moral sense. Here, too, involving children in battles means acting from a place of wholeness and responsibility—not from our woundedness, the place where we have been hurt and shattered. Even revealing our

vulnerable points to our children, if done with intention and awareness, can become part of this wholeness. By including our children
in our struggles, we strengthen our covenant with them. Together
we are part of the human search for justice. Together we can change
the world.

BOOKS AND AUTHORS MENTIONED IN "THE VILLAGE WAY"

Jean Améry, (b. Hans Mayer, 1912–1978). *At the Mind's Limits: Contemplations by a Survivor of Auschwitz and Its Realities*. Trans. Sidney and Stella P. Rosenfeld. Bloomington: Indiana University Press, 1980.

Samuel Hugo Bergman (1883-1975) was a Czech-born, German and Israeli Jewish philosopher and educator who taught at the Hebrew University in Jerusalem, Israel. His books include *Faith and Reason: An Introduction to Modern Jewish Thought* (1961).

Pierre Bertaux (1907-1986), *Mutation der Menschheit—Diagnosen und Prognosen*, Frankfurt am Main, 1963.

John Bowlby (1907-1990) was a British psychoanalytic theorist and a researcher into human emotional development. Among his important works is *Attachment and Loss* (1973).

Martin Buber (1878-1965) was a renowned Austrian born Jewish philosopher, theologian, writer and educator. Among his many books are *I and Thou* (1923) and *Paths in Utopia* (1946).

John Dewey (1859-1852) was an American philosopher, psychologist and educational reformer, and is recognized as one of the founders of the philosophical school called Pragmatism. Among his important books are *Human Nature and Conduct* (1922) and *Freedom and Culture* (1939).

Jonathan Franzen (1959-) is an American fiction writer. His book *The Corrections* won a National Book Award in 2002.

Rabbi Abraham Joshua Heschel (1907-1972) *God in search of man: a philosophy of Judaism*, Farrar, Straus & Cudahy, 1955.

Franz Kafka (1883-1924) is widely considered among the greatest German-language writers of the 20th century. His works, published posthumously, include *The Trial* (1925) and *The Castle* (1926).

George B. Leonard (1923-) is an American journalist, writer, and a leader of the human potential movement. Among his books are *The Decline of the American Male* (1958) and *Education and Ecstasy* (1968).

Kurt Zadek Lewin (1890-1947) *Field Theory in Social Science: Selected Theoretical Papers*, Harper, 1951.

Margaret Mahler (1897-1985) was a Hungarian child psychologist and psychoanalyst who made important contributions to the theory of child development.

Ian McEwan (1948-) is a British novelist. His book *Amsterdam* won the Booker prize in 1998. His other works include *A Child in Time* (1987), *Atonement* (2001) and *Saturday* (2005).

A.S. Neill (1883-1973) was a Scottish educator and founder of the Summerhill School in 1924. His book *Summerhill: A Radical Approach to Child Rearing* (1960) became an international best seller.

Neil Postman (1931-2003) was an American educator, media theorist and cultural critic. His books include *Teaching as a Subversive Activity* (1969), *Technopoly: The Surrender of Culture to Technology* (1992) and *The End of Education: Redefining the Value of School* (1995).

Gershom Scholem (1876-1982) was a German-born, Jewish philosopher and historian, and the founder of modern academic research into *Kabbala* and Jewish Mysticism. Among his books are *Major Trends in Jewish Mysticism* (1941) and *The Messianic Idea in Judaism* (1971).

Donald Winnicott (1896-1971) was an English pediatrician, psychoanalyst and one of the most influential psychological theorists of the 20th century.

ACKNOWLEDGEMENTS

This book would not have materialized without the support and encouragement of Henry and Edith Everett. Henry strongly believed that the story of Yemin Orde should be told. And indeed, after his painful passing, Edith made sure this happened. Micha Odenheimer—writer, social activist and true friend—was the catalyst in the process of writing the book, and Chanan Tigay went over the text, adding clarity where needed. The reality described in this book would not have come into existence without the American Friends of Yemin Orde and its devoted board members. Special gratitude goes to the children, now grownups, whose stories are told here, albeit with identities disguised. The warmth of their reactions when again encountering their young-old selves was a teaching in itself.

Chaim Peri

INDEX

A